WALKING TOGETHER

WALKING TOGETHER

*Roman Catholics and Ecumenism
Twenty-five Years after
Vatican II*

Edited by

Thaddeus D. Horgan

WILLIAM B. EERDMANS PUBLISHING COMPANY
GRAND RAPIDS, MICHIGAN

Copyright © 1990 by Wm. B. Eerdmans Publishing Co.
255 Jefferson Ave. S.E., Grand Rapids, Mich. 49503
All rights reserved

Printed in the United States of America

Library of Congress Cataloging-in-Publication Data

Walking together: Roman Catholics and ecumenism twenty-five years
    after Vatican II / edited by Thaddeus D. Horgan.
       p.   cm.
   ISBN (invalid) 0-8028-0475-6 (pbk.)
    1. Vatican Council (2nd: 1962-1965). Decretum de oecumenismo.
  2. Catholic Church—Relations.   3. Christian union—Catholic Church.
  I. Horgan, Thaddeus D. (Thaddeus Daniel)
  BX1784.W34   1990
  282—dc20   90-45869
                                     CIP

In Memory

Albert C. Outler
1908 – 1989

Christian theologian in the United Methodist tradition;
advocate for Christian unity;
Protestant observer at the Second Vatican Council

Contents

vii

Introduction

The Second Vatican Council was among the most momentous religious events of the twentieth century. In 1959 Pope John XXIII announced that he was calling a council into session in order to "update" the Roman Catholic Church. The results have led to great changes—many would say turmoil—within that church. Taking the long view of history, other observers will note that after every church council controversies have ensued over the decisions the council made. Only over time do we begin to see whether the results of those decisions are the ones the council anticipated or other, surprising, results. Twenty-five years have now passed since Vatican II (1962-1965). It is time for an assessment of the council's decisions. This volume records several such assessments, but they deal with only one of the council's concerns: the Roman Catholic Church's relationship to Christians in other churches and its efforts toward Christian unity.

The council's document that treated these issues is popularly known as the Decree on Ecumenism promulgated by Pope Paul VI on November 21, 1964. Beginning in November 1989 and continuing through symposia held during the spring of 1990, several lectures and other addresses were delivered in the

United States to evaluate the Roman Catholic Church's involvement in interchurch activities and its efforts to restore unity among divided Christians. Christians of a variety of traditions deeply committed to the fulfillment of the prayer of Christ "that they may all be one . . . that the world may know" (John 17:21, 23), and not Roman Catholics alone, are looking at that church's commitment in deed as well as in speech. Since 60 percent of the world's Christians are Roman Catholics, Christian unity, if it is to be actual, must include Catholics. Other Christians—not just Catholics—are concerned that the reforms launched by the council have been authentic. They are concerned that the steps taken by the Roman Catholic Church toward reconciliation with other churches are genuine. This concern should be borne in mind as the reader considers the assessments and suggestions contained in the papers presented here.

The first set of six papers were delivered at a symposium held in Washington, D.C., in November 1989, cosponsored by the Graymoor Franciscan Friars of the Atonement, an American Roman Catholic religious order dedicated to promoting Christian unity, and by the Institute for Ecumenics of the Washington Theological Consortium, a cluster of theological schools located in the area of the national capital. The program was developed in cooperation with the Secretariat for Ecumenical and Inter-Religious Affairs of the National Conference of Catholic Bishops. The Reverend Thaddeus Horgan, S.A., from that office and United Methodist theologian Rev. Dr. David Trickett, director of the consortium, organized the program.

The other papers were prepared for a special issue of the Graymoor Ecumenical Institute's publication *Ecumenical Trends* and for symposia held in Bridgeport, Cleveland, and Los Angeles. Archbishop J. Francis Stafford's and Dr. Thomas Hoyt's papers were read in the context of worship services held respectively in the National Shrine of the Immaculate Conception and in the chapel of the interdenominational Howard Divinity School, both in Washington, D.C.

One matter on which all Christians agree, because of the example of Christ, is that prayer is essential to every effort at reconciliation among Christians. At each of the events where these papers were delivered, all the participants shared in prayer. One of these prayers, offered at the Washington symposium, sums up how the writers of these papers generally assess the overall movement toward Christian unity.

> Come Holy Spirit of Pentecost, who enabled the apostles to
>   announce the wonders of salvation;
> Lead us to unity so the world may believe.
>
> Come Holy Spirit who led the deacon Philip on the road
>   from Gaza;
> Teach us to know and share the truth of the good news.
>
> Come Holy Spirit present at the Council of Jerusalem;
> Gather all Christians together in love,
> And unite the churches in the bond of peace.
>
> O God, source of all being and life,
> In giving us the Spirit of your Son
> Pour into our hearts the fullness of truth and love
> So that we might be strengthened to continue to fulfill
> The prayer of your Son
> That all be one.

TDH

The Decree on Ecumenism and the Challenge of the Future

Arthur A. Vogel

Christians are meant to be a celebrating people; they celebrate by coming together, and they celebrate what brings them together. As St. Paul indicated in his second letter to the Corinthians, Christians are both a reconciled and reconciling people; they have been reconciled to God through Christ, and, as ambassadors of Christ, they have been given a ministry of reconciliation in the world (2 Cor. 5:18)

Christ is not divided and neither should his disciples be, as Paul wrote in his first letter to the Corinthians (1:13). In his letter to the Ephesians, Paul's understanding of the unity God intends in Christ is all-inclusive. Paul says that the Father had purposed in Christ "a plan for the fulness of time, to unite *all* things in him, things in heaven and things on earth" (1:9-10).

It is appropriate that we celebrate the twenty-fifth anniversary of the Decree on Ecumenism. In that document, and in the spirit that produced it, the Second Vatican Council recog-

Arthur A. Vogel is the Episcopal Church's retired Bishop of Western Missouri. He has served on the original and serves on the current Anglican-Roman Catholic International Commissions (ARCIC I, II).

1

nized with new insight the reconciliation and oneness God gives his people. The community of reconciliation brought about by Christ was recognized in a new way by a community among communities.

Searching for a metaphor to describe the effects of the Second Vatican Council in general, and the Decree on Ecumenism in particular, I am tempted to describe the conciliar event as a rocket shot into the sky illuminating areas of Christian life with new light and understanding. The analogy is not a good one, however, for we all know that once a skyrocket has exploded it is completely burned out, leaving only a few dead ashes to float back to earth. A better analogy might be to describe Vatican II as a blastema, a new beginning of life that is meant to be followed by ongoing growth and differentiation. Let us see how the blastema of Vatican II came about and how it has begun to grow, briefly charting the course of its life up to this point.

The announcement of a Second Vatican Council was somewhat unexpected, but, as with any birth, there was preparation for it. The offspring brought forth by the labor of the council still surprised many people. There were those who had hoped for new dogmatic definitions from the council, perhaps that Mary would be declared *mediatrix et fons* of all grace; others, formed by an ecclesiology of the manuals, hoped that the council would advance the cause of Christian unity by no more difficult a method than issuing a more graciously worded invitation to the "separated brethren" to "return home" to the Roman Catholic Church. But those who thought the preparation for the council would produce these expected results were to be surprised.

Assessing the work of the council at our current distance, it is clear that the most telling preparation for it occurred in the 1950s and '60s when modern critical methods of studying and interpreting the Scriptures came to be shared by the Roman Catholic Church with the other Christian churches in the world. The study of Scripture, once a point of conflict, became a means of cooperation, and there was an increasing emphasis on the importance of Scripture as the norm of Christian experience of God. The study of patristics advanced with the study of Scripture, and both the theological and liturgical lives of the Roman Catholic Church were changed and enriched as a result. Theology was released from its abstract essentialistic imprisonment, and movement was rediscovered to be normal in liturgy. When the Word became flesh, Truth somehow entered history and became temporal. In that light Roman Catholics theologians saw that historical location and limitation were constitutive elements of theology, not elements of its destruction. In 1950 Roman Catholics began to participate in the ecumenical Old Testament Society, and later participated in ecumenical organizations devoted to New Testament studies. Roman Catholics attended the first international Patristic Conference at Oxford in 1952, and Roman Catholic consultants helped plan the Second Assembly of the World Council of Churches, which met in Evanston in 1954.

The pontificate of John XXIII did not look for surprise. He was conservative in his spirituality and in his theology, but a Christian leader who says that any day is a good day to be born or to die touches a common ground of faith that transcends theological schools and positions. John was undeniably conservative. Shortly before the council, he issued an encyclical requiring that theology be taught in Latin in all the seminaries of the church, and he dedicated his revolutionary council to God at the shrine of our Lady of Loretto. Nevertheless John XXIII also saw the need to proclaim the Christian faith in a manner that better communicated with the contemporary world, and his desire for *aggiornamento* led to the calling of an "Ecumenical Council of the Universal Church" in the first year of his pontificate.

Pope John continued to surprise when, in 1959, he announced that separated communities were to be invited to join in a common search for unity. In 1960 he established the Secretariat for the Promotion of Christian Unity, with future cardinals Bea as its president and Willebrands as its secretary.

My assignment is to assess rather than to describe, but we must recall a few actions of the council that began to give structure to the Roman Catholic Church's new relations with other Christian churches and communities. The whole Christian world was gratified by the council's affirmation of the collegial nature of life in the church, by its acknowledgment that every baptized person is somehow identified with the visible church, that the church of Christ is no longer simply to be identified with the Roman Catholic Church in that church's theology, and that the Virgin Mary is to be acknowledged in a biblical, patristic, and ecclesiological context. Important ground was gained when the council denied the two-source theory of revelation.

The Decree on Ecumenism opened the Roman Catholic Church in a new manner to the wider Christian community when it stated that the Holy Spirit, the principle of the church's unity, uses "separated Churches . . . as means of salvation" (chap. 1, par. 3). That the holy eucharist is both a sign and cause of unity, that the church is a pilgrim church in the world, that there is a hierarchy of truths, and that ecumenism requires "a change of heart" are important truths for all Christians reaffirmed in the Decree. Another significant truth is found in the statement that the more the faithful live according to the gospel, the more they are fostering and even practicing Christian unity (chap. 2, par. 7). The spiritual water from that well may have yet to be tasted, if not discovered, by many people who count themselves members of the pilgrim church, but who are too weary in their local congregations to have a concern for wider church unity.

Closer to the present time, some remarks by Pope John Paul II on the occasion of another twenty-fifth anniversary, that of the Secretariat (now the Pontifical Council) for Promoting Christian Unity, measure the development of the blastema to which we previously referred—and they provide a basis for identifying challenges for the future.

Addressing the Roman Curia on that anniversary in June of 1985, John Paul noted the theological dialogue that was being carried on by the Roman Catholic Church with the churches of the East and West. He went on to "reaffirm that the Catholic Church is committed to the ecumenical movement with an irrevocable decision" and that his "Petrine ministry . . . is at the service of unity in truth and charity."

A constant note sounded in all the ecumenical dialogue involving the Roman Catholic Church was reiterated in the pope's statement that "unity in the profession of faith is the fundamental element in the manifestation of ecclesial communion." Referring to the "faith once for all delivered to the saints" (Jude 3), the pope significantly added that "this truth is neither abstract nor academic." In several places in the address, the pope stated that reestablishing Christian unity was among his pastoral priorities, and he reiterated that the Spirit, "the profound source of unity," is "an eschatological gift to the Church." The eschatological nature of the gift of the Spirit is a factor in the life of the church to which, I believe, we must give increased attention in our journey toward the visible reunion of the church.

The Roman Catholic Church is presently engaged in national and international dialogues with almost all the major denominations of the East and West; a number of those dialogues began before the conclusion of Vatican II. What challenge for the future does such involvement offer? Each dialogue has problems and accomplishments of its own which reach into the future, but the introductory nature of my assessment here will not allow me to mine material from so many locations. Because of the nature of the Roman Catholic Church, however, a number of common themes run throughout the dialogues, and I will discuss those that I believe have major importance.

In some instances, the challenge to the Roman Catholic Church is to make more clear its self-understanding and its level of acceptance of the actions of Vatican II; in other instances the challenge is to grow with other churches in a life in Christ that is already shared and held in common. This division of themes should not be taken as an ultimate bifurcation, however, for none of us—either as individuals or in community—has a Christian identity apart from our relation to others and apart from the *koinonia* we have in Christ, which is the basis for our communion with each other.

Before we proceed to the challenges of the future, we must express gratitude for the newness of the future that has been opened up by many of the graceful insights of Vatican II and by the development of the embryonic life that first saw light as the Decree on Ecumenism. All Christian churches rejoice in the growth in wider community made possible by the actions of Vatican II, and they are grateful for the enrichment of our common life in Christ made possible by the heritage of the Roman Catholic Church.

A first principle in the quest for a unified church is that "unity" does not mean "uniformity." The unity of the church must be truly "catholic," that is, it must be a rich unity universally embracing the diversity of local churches with their special gifts and riches. As Cardinal Willebrands stated in a famous sermon preached in Cambridge in 1970, a united church of Christ must contain different "types" *(typoi)* within it.

There is an increasing consensus being achieved through the dialogues, I believe (although this view is not universally accepted), that the visible unity of the church (the latter conceived as a communion of communities) is most adequately revealed to the world if the unity is visibly focused in a primate who is a servant of the unity within the *koinonia*. A growing number of people, I also believe, are now prepared to say that the most logical person to be such a primate and servant of unity is the Bishop of Rome. Even in the divided church, no one has wider acceptance as the spokesman for all Christian people than the Bishop of Rome.

Historical development alone offers the pope as the most logical person to serve as primate of the universal church. Those non-Catholics who are willing to accept the pope in such a role are those that read the historical development of the primacy of the see of Rome as a mark of providence. Roman Catholic theology has traditionally argued for papal primacy on the basis of "divine right." A major theological problem still to be resolved in the future is to determine, if there is to be a universal primate of the church, whether that ministry is *jure divino, divina providentia,* or *ordinatio divina.* Do the terms convey irreconcilable theological differences, or, for the sake of the unity and mission of the church, can a common mind be found among them?

Vatican II stressed the collegial nature of life in the church, and describing the church as a *koinonia* is one of the most commonly accepted themes in the various bilateral and multilateral dialogues going on today. Granted all that we have said up to this point, it is also a historical fact, as Avery Dulles has so effectively pointed out, that the Western Church, centered in Rome at the heart of the Roman Empire, came to adopt the model of the political state as its administrative model. In that model, unity *does* tend toward uniformity. Thus, in the life of the Roman Catholic Church after Vatican II, we find a tension (would it be too much to say a struggle?) between uniformity and pluriformity, between primacy and conciliarity/collegiality, between the focus of unity and dispersed authority. While the tests of Vatican II stand and the synod of bishops established by Paul VI exists and episcopal conferences are in place in the Roman Catholic Church, one does not find the correlation and interdependence among these entities that the collegial statements of Vatican II lead one to expect. How will collegial oversight develop in the ongoing life of the Roman Catholic Church? That is a challenge for the future.

Understanding the church as the people of God brings up the roles of laity in the church, a challenge of the understanding and life of all Christians today. Baptized into the high priesthood of Christ, the members of the church exist as a royal priesthood in the world. All the churches are challenged to grow in such self-understanding. In the Roman Catholic Church such growth will manifest itself in a more balanced and clarified collegiality between what has traditionally been called the "teaching" and the "learning" church. Those terms no longer can be—and never properly were—equated with "clergy" and "laity" respectively.

The role of women in the church and the issue of the ordination of women must be mentioned here. This is an area the churches must explore together. Churches that do and churches that do not ordain women justify their positions on the basis of revelation, new life in Christ, and the fulfillment of God's purpose. Here is an area in which the churches need deep dialogue about their understanding of Christology and eschatology and the effects of those subjects upon the nature of ordained ministry. What kind of representation of Christ is made in an ordained minister?

Several bilateral dialogues have agreed that Peter held a special position among the twelve apostles, but there is no necessary admission in that fact that Peter held a primacy that was to be transmitted to successors. There has, nevertheless, been growth in the acceptance of the need for a ministry in the church today that is *analogous* to the role of Peter in the band of twelve. There is a special challenge to the Bishop of Rome, therefore, so to exercise a Petrine ministry within the Roman Catholic Church that other churches will see its necessity and desire its benefits.

"Infallibility" is a subject that must take its place in a catalog such as this. It is a concept that the church got along without for twelve centuries, and it is a concept that has afflicted the church with misunderstanding since its introduction. Aware of the formal theological arguments made for it, one may hope that a future reconciliation of its meaning with the concept of "indefectibility" will not be impossible, for the only empirical criterion that an infallible judgment has been made amounts to the indefectibility of the judgment's reception by the church.

Cultural relativity within the church offers both a challenge and an opportunity for the future. The Roman Catholic Church is by far the largest single worldwide Christian church; other worldwide churches are actually worldwide communions or associations of autocephalous churches. The single administration of such a diverse community of communities as the Roman Catholic Church, and the penchant for good order historically characteristic of Rome in all of its activities, should help non-Roman Catholics appreciate the difficulty with which the Bishop of Rome is faced both canonically and theologically in his oversight of the church. Granted the different canonical structures of the churches of the world, it may nevertheless be asked if, for the ultimate good of the united church, communion may not be advanced in different degrees in different locations as opportunities arise.

The summary challenge of the future, it seems to me, for all churches engaged in dialogue about unity with the Roman Catholic Church is to discover and actualize the dynamics of the church as a Spirit-filled body whose visible unity is centered and focused in a person whose role and ministry is at one time to witness to what the body already is and to call it to what it ought to be doing in its mission to the world. I believe the statement just made is a description of what a bishop ought to be in a diocese—and what the primate in a universal church is called to be. In such a dynamic we need what may be called an *ecological ecclesiology*, one that will keep all aspects of Christian community in balance, not losing sight of the interconnectedness and interdependence of all things Christian—and indeed of all things. That is challenge enough for anyone.

Ecclesiology should be the ultimate synthesizing perspective in Christian theology. Accordingly, in the search for the unity of the church, theological decisions must not be based on narrow ecclesiological and canonical positions. In the last chapter of the Dogmatic Constitution on Divine Revelation, Scripture is said to be "the soul of sacred theology." We have seen that cooperative interchurch study of Scripture was a most important preparation for the blastema of Vatican II. Might it not be the case that a conscious return to the study of the scriptural sources we all have in common could supply the common insight we need to move us beyond our present difficulties?

The nature and exercise of authority in the church is ultimately the most vexing problem we face in the reunification of the church. I am aware of no treatment of authority in the church that does not begin with the profession that all Christian authority derives from God the Father through Christ. All Christian authority is Christ's. The word "Christ," however, connotes a nature and an office that can be propositionally

defined: it means "anointed one." But the Christ in whom
Christians find salvation is not just an example of an abstract
definition; he is the unique, singular, and mysterious man from
Nazareth, Jesus. Truth entered time in the incarnation, we
previously said, and that Truth is inseparable from the historical
man Jesus. Authority tends to be exercised differently in the
name of Christ, I suggest, than it is in the name of Jesus:
authority in the former instance might be no more than a
proposition formally deduced from another proposition, but
authority in the second instance is located in a historically
circumscribed man recognized to be mysteriously filled with the
Spirit of God. Ecclesiology, if it is fully Christian, must not be
isolated from the historic life of Jesus himself. That means the
renewed quest for the historical Jesus in contemporary scriptural studies must not be separated from the ecclesiology of
church reunion. The church as the Spirit-filled body of Christ
in the world depends so totally on the man from Nazareth,
Jesus, in whom "the whole fulness of deity dwells bodily" (Col.
2:9), that we must not allow the propositional authority of the
mystical body to outstrip the lived authority of its head and
source. Christians know no Christ apart from Jesus; the church
is a community of witness to him, not a successor that surpasses
him. In nothing less than total dependence upon him we
humbly and repentantly seek unity in his name.

Because Christ Jesus is undivided the church cannot
remain divided without disobedience to him; thus to be a
Christian is to have the duty of church unity, as Karl Rahner
has stressed. Certainly the Decree on Ecumenism was correct
when it stated that all who live according to the gospel must, by
that very fact, be practicing Christian unity. Such living is our
challenge for the future.

Response to Arthur Vogel

Donald J. Reece

This response is shaped by "social ecumenism" instead of "dialogic" or "doctrinal ecumenism." By "social ecumenism" I mean an ecumenical climate of praxis: where Roman Catholics rub elbows at all levels with Protestants in "common witness"; where Roman Catholics are founding members of the Regional Caribbean Conference of Churches (CCC); where they are active members of local Christian councils; where they conduct services in Protestant churches; where they have a deep love for the Bible; and where they literally go to bed with Protestants due to the preponderance of mixed marriages. Notwithstanding all of that, ecumenical dialogues in the strict sense do not abound in the territories of the Caribbean. Yet theologically there are Caribbean people making a mark at the World Council of Churches and participating in international bilateral and multilateral conversations. When asked to make this response to Bishop Vogel's paper, which is so full of ecumenical chal-

Donald J. Reece is the Roman Catholic Bishop of St. John's-Basseterre, Antigua, West Indies, and a member of the Pontifical Council for Promoting Christian Unity.

11

lenges, I had to restudy several Vatican II documents—so
conditioned am I by "social ecumenism"!

I commend the bishop for the way he commenced his
presentation. Quoting St. Paul, he says that Christians "have
been given a ministry of reconciliation in the world" (2 Cor.
5:18). The fact that we have been entrusted with this ministry,
and that John 17:21 tells us that unity is for mission, should
convince us that ecumenism is not an option for Christians.
Hence the Decree on Ecumenism has come to be considered
a watershed for the formation of Roman Catholics as they
enter more fully into the field of interchurch relations. I am
convinced that it was truly inspired by the Holy Spirit who is
the soul of the ecumenical movement, the One who makes us
one.

Bishop Vogel rightly shifts from the imagery of an illuminating (yet fading) rocket to the imagery of a blastema to
suggest growth and evolution. The mystery of God's design
for unity cannot always be planned or predicted. This is a
healthy reminder to those of us with a Western mentality.
Often we think that we can program ourselves to attain our
goals. Personally I would have employed another image, that
of two persons going steady with marriage ultimately in mind.
Here not only the mystery of attraction and love is present but
also the need to grow together through frank communication—not excluding hurts and misunderstanding—that can
result in a healthy, lasting union forever deepening and developing.

In listing some of the positive ecumenical effects of the
Second Vatican Council, Bishop Vogel states, *inter alia,* that
"important ground was gained when the council denied the
two-source theory of revelation." I feel "denied" is too strong a
term. In Chapter II of the Dogmatic Constitution on Divine
Revelation, one reads: "Sacred Tradition and sacred Scripture,
then, are bound closely together, and communicate one with
the other. For both of them, flowing out from the same divine
well-spring, come together in some fashion to form one thing,
and move towards the same goal" (9).

To assert that the council denied tradition could resurrect for some Roman Catholics the old Protestant issue of *sola scriptura*. On the other hand, the bishop is mindful of the preeminent position tradition held in Catholic thinking and practice prior to Vatican II. It can be asserted, however, that the council moved Catholics away from a "two-source theory" when it spoke of the experience of and handing on of the central truth of Christian faith, God's revelation in Jesus Christ.

Ecumenical Events to Date

Any assessment of the twenty-five years since the publication of the Decree on Ecumenism should stress the concept of "spiritual ecumenism." Without prayer and a conversion of heart there can be no genuine or enduring Christian unity. I would have liked to have heard in Bishop Vogel's remarks some mention of the 1986 Assisi gathering where the pope, Archbishop Runcie, and other spiritual leaders prayed for world peace. And what of the various prayer movements of our day, like the Charismatic Renewal in which Catholics, Anglicans, and other Protestants participate.

Other positive developments that might have been mentioned are:

1. The ground-breaking meeting between Pope Paul VI and Eastern Orthodox Patriarch Athenagoras I. In a *Common Declaration* they expressed regret for the offenses the churches committed against one another in the past as well as their intent to "erase from memory and the midst of the Church the sentences of excommunication which followed them." By their historic declaration they committed their churches to work for the restoration of "full communion of faith, brotherly accord and sacramental life" (December 7, 1965). A second *Common Declaration* and exchange of visits between the pope and ecumenical patriarch took place in 1967. Their successors, John Paul II and Demetrius I, likewise exchange visits and twice

issued *Common Declarations,* in 1979 and in 1987. Each year on the feasts of the Ss. Peter and Paul and of St. Andrew the heads of these churches exchange greetings and send delegations to one another's celebrations.

2. *The Joint Declaration on Cooperation* by Pope Paul IV and Archbishop Michael Ramsey of Canterbury in which they wished "to leave in the hands of God of mercy all that in the past has been opposed to the precept of charity," and intended "to inaugurate between the Roman Catholic Church and the Anglican Communion a serious dialogue which, founded on the Gospels and on the ancient common traditions, may lead to that unity of truth, for which Christ prayed" (March 24, 1966).

3. The meeting of Pope Paul VI and Vasken I, Catholicos and Supreme Patriarch of the Armenians. Their *Common Declaration* invited the faithful of their churches to "respond with greater fidelity to the call of the Holy Spirit stimulating them to a more profound unity" (May 12, 1970). This was the beginning of a series, four in all, of visits and *Common Declarations* between the Roman Pontiff and the heads of the Oriental (Syrian, Armenian, and Coptic) Orthodox Churches.

4. The meeting of Pope Paul VI and Dr. Runcie's predecessor as Archbishop of Canterbury, Donald Coggin. In their *Common Declaration* they called for greater cooperation between Anglicans and Roman Catholics since such cooperation "is the true setting for continued dialogue and for the general extension and appreciation of its fruits, and so for progress towards that goal which is Christ's will—the restoration of complete communion in faith and sacramental life" (April 29, 1977).

5. Fresh in our minds, of course, is the most recent (1989) meeting between Pope John Paul II and Archbishop Robert Runcie of Canterbury when the latter returned the Pope's 1982 visit to Canterbury. They reiterated their intention to continue on the pilgrimage toward unity despite seemingly insurmountable obstacles on both sides (the ordination of a woman to the episcopacy for Catholics and papal primacy for Anglicans).

Future Challenges

Among the challenges for the future, Bishop Vogel focuses on the national and international dialogues that are taking place "with almost all of the major denominations of the East and West." He wonders what lies ahead as a result of these dialogues. This is a legitimate query. Because people cannot seriously engage in dialogue without being changed, introspection and self-understanding for a change of heart must be by-products of those dialogues. But the results of dialogue must go further. How far is the issue? And how extensive has the influence of dialogue been? Has it touched the rank and file in our churches? This is a real pastoral concern. Are we going to prevent a replay of the Council of Florence (1439)? On that occasion church leaders, East and West, forged a unity. But they faced nonacceptance when they returned to their ecclesiastical jurisdictions. It could happen again. Ecumenism has to engage all in our churches.

Currently in many parts of the world local Catholic and Protestant communities are grappling with their own identity in the face of indigenization. In these areas ecumenism is not viewed as a necessity, but as a problem. This self-identity question is exacerbated further in Latin America and the Caribbean by the forceful proselytizing tactics of some sects and fundamentalist groups. This too needs to be addressed and not glossed over.

For Bishop Vogel the most crucial challenge is the thorny matter of church authority. How is authority exercised, especially with reference to the local church? What is its role in face of collegiality? While these are grave concerns to the Orthodox Churches and the Anglican Communion, they equally are a primary concern for Roman Catholics. In many dioceses different cultures, traditions, and particular local circumstances shape the way authority is exercised. If genuine catholicity is to become a reality, then that theoretic latitude for diversity must be allowed concrete expression.

By advocating this, I do not imply that the Petrine ministry, so necessary for Christian unity, should be emasculated. As a Catholic I could never accept a pope merely as chairman of a board of church leaders. When one attends the Synod of Bishops in Rome, as I have, and experiences the diversity of ecclesiologies, one appreciates the value and importance of the Petrine ministry. The pope presides "in love" as the "servant of the servants of God" for the sake of unity.

The issue of the role of women in the church is now of greater importance to our two communions. With Bishop Vogel I propose that in both our traditions a deeper understanding of Christology and eschatology is needed. But I wonder where and how this might be dealt with ecumenically. In dialogues? Or in our own particular theological dens? Should it be treated as a matter of revelation or merely as a question of custom or discipline? I do not feel that its resolution is to be achieved by decisions of autonomous provinces. Let us remember that this is a matter that involves half the membership of the universal church.

This, as well as several other of Bishop Vogel's challenges, are like mines in the apparent green field of ecumenism. His great concern is the authority question. I have some difficulty with his nuances of patterning church authority on the historical Jesus instead of on the Christ of faith. Is this calling for at least four different expressions of church authority dependent on the people served or addressed? One does not want to say this won't be a way forward, but I feel it needs much discussion and greater theological clarification before it could be considered operative.

Because of the Holy Spirit's vital role in our efforts to realize the priestly prayer of Jesus, the most important element to press ahead with is spiritual ecumenism. It is only then that each church, like spokes in a bicycle wheel, will move closer to each other as they move toward the hub who is Christ Jesus himself. In Christ, by the Spirit's power, Christians will achieve unity. Persistent and faithful promoters, like Bishop Vogel who roots himself in Christ, give us that confident hope.

The Decree on Ecumenism:
Twenty-five Years After

Avery Dulles, S.J.

Beyond reasonable doubt, the Decree on Ecumenism, *Unitatis redintegratio,* was one of the principal achievements of the Second Vatican Council. Compact and precisely worded, it shines like a jewel among the council documents. By its cogent reasoning it carried the Catholic Church out of its previous isolation and plunged it into the mainstream of the ecumenical movement. Firmly and loyally Catholic, the decree was nevertheless fair and optimistic in its appreciation of the authentic heritage of Orthodox, Anglican, and Protestant Christianity.

Unitatis redintegratio clearly designated the goal of the ecumenical movement as full visible unity. While recognizing that this goal was far distant and, indeed, beyond human control, the decree made it evident that a very important measure of unity already exists. The things that unite Christians, it suggested, are at least as important as those that divide them. The proximate goal of ecumenism is to increase the

Avery Dulles, S.J., is the McGinley Professor of Religion and Science at Fordham University, Bronx, N.Y., and a member of both the international and national Lutheran-Roman Catholic Dialogues.

partial or imperfect communion that now obtains. The practice of ecumenism accordingly aims at a gradual increase of common worship, common witness, and common service. To make such advances possible the Decree called for spiritual ecumenism and theological dialogue. The dialogue, conducted by competent experts, must avoid all false irenicism. In other words, it must realistically acknowledge the barriers that still exist.

Ever since Vatican II the Catholic Church has participated in ecumenism, under the encouraging leadership of the popes and the Secretariat for Promoting the Unity of Christians (recently reclassified as a council rather than a secretariat). In the present pontificate this participation remains lively. The celebration in 1980 of the 450th anniversary of the Augsburg Confession and in 1983 of the 500th anniversary of Luther's birth, as well as the visits exchanged between the pope, the ecumenical patriarch of Constantinople, and the Archbishop of Canterbury are powerful tokens of this continuing vitality.

In the United States the Catholic Church has been officially involved in eleven sets of ecumenical consultations sponsored by the National Conference of Catholic Bishops' Secretariat for Ecumenical and Interreligious Affairs. The most active of these consultations have been with the Lutherans, the Orthodox, and the Episcopalians. The Catholic Church plays a prominent role in the Faith and Order Commission of the National Council of Christian Churches, which has as its executive director Brother Jeffrey Gros, F.S.C. Flourishing centers of ecumenical research exist at Graymoor on Hudson, at Collegeville, Minnesota, and at Belmont Abbey, North Carolina, to mention only three. Many theological schools and seminaries belong to ecumenical consortia, such as the one here in Washington.

The practical aspects of ecumenism are regularly studied under the auspices of the National Association of Diocesan Ecumenical Officers, which annually meets with the Episcopal Diocesan Ecumenical Officers and other denominational ecumenical representatives at the National Workshop on Christian

Unity. Many dioceses and parishes are involved in covenants with Lutherans and Anglicans. In 1990, 76 of the 187 Roman Catholic dioceses in the country were members of state councils of churches. In view of developments such as these it is unwarranted to speak, as some do, of ecumenical stagnation.

Since 1964 the communion model of ecumenism, espoused in the documents of Vatican II, has won increasing acceptance throughout the Christian world. The goal of the ecumenical movement is seen as the establishment or restoration of full communion among separated Christian groups, each of which is in full communion with its own members. The Extraordinary Synod of Bishops in 1985 reaffirmed this vision of ecumenism. "We bishops ardently desire that the incomplete communion already existing with the non-Catholic churches and communities might, with the grace of God, come to the point of full communion" (Final Report II C 7).

A similar theology of communion is accepted by many other Christian bodies. Long before Vatican II, Anglicanism depicted itself as a communion seeking full fellowship with other Christian churches. The Orthodox have repeatedly asserted that the *una sancta* is essentially a communion of churches. At Budapest in 1984 the Lutheran World Federation spoke explicitly of the "Lutheran communion of churches." The Roman Catholic-Lutheran Joint Commission in its statement "Facing Unity" (1984) took its departure from the idea that the Church is a *communio* subsisting in a network of local churches (no. 5). From Vatican II this statement took over the idea that *communio* consists of three elements: confession of the same apostolic faith, participation in the same sacramental life, and fellowship in ministry and service.

In the United States the proposed Church of Christ Uniting (hitherto known as the Consultation on Church Union) has recently adopted the communion vision of unity. According to the plan drawn up in 1988 it aspires to be not a new denomination but a "covenant communion of churches." Instead of separating the member churches from their parent bodies, the proposed church may perhaps serve as a catalyst drawing those bodies closer together. If it adheres consistently to this vision, the Church of Christ Uniting may be more attractive to members of "world confessional families," Anglican, Presbyterian, Methodist, and perhaps eventually Lutheran as well. The resulting covenant communion may present the Catholic Church with new challenges and new opportunities.

The theological dialogues recommended by Vatican II have borne fruit beyond all expectation. On the international level, ARCIC (Anglican-Roman Catholic International Commission) and the Roman Catholic-Lutheran Joint Commission have produced dialogue statements of major importance. The Groupe des Dombes in France and the Lutheran-Catholic dialogue in Germany have been highly successful. The Lutheran-Catholic dialogue in the United States has generated splendid series of volumes on topics such as the Nicene Creed, baptism, the eucharist, ministry, papal primacy, teaching authority in the church, and justification by faith. The results of the various bilateral conversations have fed back into the Faith and Order Commission of the World Council of Churches, notably in the Lima Document (BEM) of 1982, which gave classic formulation to the striking convergences on Baptism, Eucharist, and Ministry that had been shaped in the previous fifty years. This document reinforced the trend in many ecumenically oriented churches to adhere to the threefold pattern of ministry—bishops, presbyters, and deacons—and to promote the historic succession of bishops as a sign and symbol of the apostolic succession of the church itself.

In the United States, the Bishops' Commission for Ecumenical Affairs submitted a basically favorable report on the Lima Document in September 1985. In a still more positive response, the Vatican Secretariat for Promoting Christian Unity in July 1987 characterized it as "perhaps the most significant result of the [Faith and Order] movement so far." But it added that in view of persisting disagreements about the apostolic succession and the ordination of women the proposals regarding the mutual recognition of ministries were premature.

In its reference to the ordination of women the Vatican Secretariat pointed to a major source of difficulty that has troubled ecumenists for the past decade or so. Firmly opposed by the Orthodox, by some Anglicans, and by many conservative evangelicals, the ordination of women to presbyterial or even episcopal office is practiced in other Anglican churches and by most mainline Protestants. The Roman Catholic Church thus far has officially opposed the practice, but it is a matter of continuing theological discussion, especially in the United States. At the present time it would be too early to judge that this issue constitutes an insuperable barrier to mutual recognition of ministries. Undoubtedly the practice has cast a shadow on the bilateral dialogues that a decade ago seemed to be on the verge of devising acceptable formulas for the validation of the ordained ministries of Protestant churches in the eyes of Roman Catholics.

Valuable and indispensable as the dialogues are, they cannot be expected by themselves to solve all problems. They can exhibit the real agreements that were always latent behind the confessional battles; they can overcome obstacles that were due to misunderstandings of one another's positions; and they can promote convergent developments within the participating communions. But as the dialogues proceed they increasingly encounter stubborn differences that do not yield to merely hermeneutical treatment. So far as can be seen at present, papal primacy of jurisdiction as defined at Vatican Council I cannot be given a meaning broadly acceptable to non-Roman Catholics. The same may be said of dogmas such as the Immaculate Conception, so far as most Protestants are concerned. Other examples could easily be added. To an increasing extent the dialogues are running up against hard-core differences on which the representatives of the churches lack both the authority and the inclination to find ways to reconcile these differences.

Accustomed as we are to the idea that dialogue ends in agreement, we can easily become impatient. Should the churches be willing to make greater sacrifices for the sake of unity? Or are there sacrifices that should not be made even for this noble goal? In a recent volume of essays, *Church, Ecumenism and Politics,* Cardinal Joseph Ratzinger has warned against the danger of transforming ecumenism into diplomacy, thereby short-circuiting the question of truth (pp. 98, 142). We must be on guard against the temptation to treat all differences as though they were matters of taste, culture, or historical conditioning. At a certain point the truth of revelation and the confessional integrity of faith communities are at stake.

The emphasis on openness and flexibility since Vatican II has produced some negative effects. The churches most involved in the ecumenical dialogues are often the least firm in their confessional witness. If they are not to lose out to unecumenical churches of a fundamentalist or pentecostal variety, the mainline churches need to recover their nerve and proffer their own witness more clearly. The Orthodox churches have on the whole done better in this respect than the mainline churches of the west.

In his 1984 address to the Budapest meeting of the Lutheran World Federation Cardinal Johannes Willebrands took note of a "reconfessionalizing" trend in the ecumenical movement. This trend would be unfortunate, he pointed out, if it meant a return to the hostile and defensive attitudes of the past, but it could be beneficial if it led to a deeper concern for the truth of doctrine and a keener realization of the need to work through the historic differences between the confessions. My own experience seems to indicate that a reconfessionalized ecumenism is on the rise, and is perhaps called for at the present stage.

If the churches do take this direction, ecumenism still remains a high priority. To be authentically confessional the churches must first of all make a common profession of their faith in the triune God and in the Incarnate Son, our redeemer. On points where their witness is divided the respective denominations must forthrightly present their own positions and respond to each other's positions. Every church can profit from listening to a clear and unambiguous presentation of the others' point of view; it stands to gain from hearing its own doctrines criticized from the perspective of outsiders. In this way individual believers can gain a deeper realization of their dependence on the communities in which their own faith has been molded; they can learn to formulate their distinctive positions more circumspectly, and they can gain a deeper appreciation for the faith of Christians belonging to other churches. In frank and respectful dialogue we can achieve a new kind of fellowship. A community of witnessing dialogue, cutting across denominational barriers, is one of the valuable fruits of modern ecumenism. The complexity of the dialogue instills a sobering realization of how far we still are from that full communion which is the ultimate goal of the ecumenical movement.

I am aware that the distinguished theologians Heinrich Fries and Karl Rahner, in their jointly authored book *Unity of the Churches: An Actual Possibility* (1983), have called for union now among all the major Christian confessions. Union, they contend, can be decreed on the basis of a common acceptance of the Scriptures and the creeds of the early church, provided that the members of each confessional church agree not to brand the dogmatic positions of the other member churches as manifestly contrary to the gospel. Such a proposal strikes me as unrealistic. Even if the various denominational churches were willing to come together on this shaky platform, the union would be unsatisfactory. The proposal would amount, in effect, to demoting all dogmas not evidently taught by the Bible and the early creeds to the status of optional opinions, not required for full communion. Such a retreat from the dogmatic developments of the past fifteen centuries strikes me as archaistic and regressive.

The Roman Catholic-Lutheran Joint Commission produced in "Facing Unity" (1984; ET 1985) a rather different proposal, which it described as "venturesome and provisional," delineating the steps by which the two communions might move into full fellowship. This proposal, as I have already mentioned, rested on the *communio* model of ecumenism. As a matter of pure theory the process envisaged here can hardly be faulted. But the proposal seems to reflect an overly sanguine view of the achievements of the dialogues. Speaking of the joint exercise of ministry, the document states: "If a fundamental consensus is reached on faith, sacramental life, and ordained ministry such that the remaining differences no longer can appear as church dividing, and reciprocal doctrinal condemnations no longer have any basis, then a mutual act of recognition should certainly follow" ("Facing Unity," no. 123). A statement of this kind may be helpful for clarifying the long-term goals of the dialogue, but it ought not to be read as reflecting the present actuality. My own impression is that the conditions set forth in this complex sentence are still far from being verified.

Under present circumstances ecumenism would do well to emphasize its proximate and intermediate goals, some of which are clearly attainable even today. The churches can gain a more accurate understanding of each other's true positions and a deeper respect for their shared commitment to the gospel. They can achieve a large measure of common witness, common worship, and common service to the world. These goals are intrinsically valuable, and should not be degraded to the status of mere means. Admittedly they fall far short of the ultimate goal of full visible unity. That goal exceeds the capacities of human effort. Here again, the Decree on Ecumenism gives valuable counsel. In its concluding paragraph we read: "This sacred Council . . . declares that it realizes that this holy objective—the reconciliation of all Christians in the unity of the one and only Church of Christ—transcends human powers and gifts. It therefore places its hope entirely in the prayer of Christ for the Church . . ." (24). Our prayer for unity ought to be more than a perfunctory ceremony. It is the divinely chosen means for attaining those blessings that can only be received as God's free gift. Martin Luther would, I presume, agree. In the last words to flow from his pen he wrote: "We are beggars. That is true."

Excessive reliance, then, should not be placed on the powers of theological ecumenism, which has been the primary subject of this paper. Theologians must do their work but they must direct their hopes elsewhere. Vatican II in its admirable decree called for a change of heart and holiness of life, along with public and private prayer for the unity of Christians. The soul of the entire ecumenical enterprise, it declared, is spiritual ecumenism. This insight is consistent with the vision of the greatest Catholic ecumenist of the present century. Yves Congar wrote in 1943 a piece of advice for Catholics that still holds for all who practice ecumenism: "I believe more than ever that the essential ecumenical activity of the Catholic Church should be to live its own life more fully and genuinely; to purify itself as far as possible, to grow in faithfulness, in good works, in depth of prayer and in union with God. In being fully herself, in the full strength of her vigor, she will develop her ecumenical power" (*Dialogue between Christians,* p. 31). If Congar is correct, all who live according to the gospel by that very fact promote the cause of ecumenism.

Response to Avery Dulles

William H. Lazareth

In his characteristically lucid, persuasive, and irenic presentation, Avery Dulles makes one central point that I mean both to endorse and to amplify from a complementary Lutheran perspective; namely, our ecumenical dependence on patience, that blessed fruit of the Holy Spirit which St. Paul lists right after love, joy, and peace (Gal. 5:22).

On the occasion of this anniversary observance of the Second Vatican Council's Decree on Ecumenism, Father Dulles exposes the sin of premature pessimism—all too common after only twenty-five years of intensive Catholic participation in the ecumenical movement—in view of the church's primary calling before God to proclaim the eternal truth of the gospel of Jesus Christ.

Commenting on Cardinal Joseph Ratzinger's similar warning against the danger of transforming ecumenism into diplomacy, Father Dulles reminds us sagely, "We must be on guard against the temptation to treat all differences as though

---

William Lazareth is Bishop of the Metropolitan New York Synod of the Evangelical Lutheran Church in America and past director of the Faith and Order Commission of the World Council of Churches.

they were matters of taste, culture, or historical conditioning. At a certain point the truth of revelation and the confessional integrity of faith communities are at stake." (Indeed, at this climactic point, this Lutheran almost expected Avery to finish dramatically: "Here I stand. I cannot do otherwise. God help me!")

The question of dogmatic truth must remain at the very heart of the ecumenical quest for full communion in the church catholic. Yet this unswerving commitment to the church's visible unity being grounded in Jesus Christ alone as "the pioneer and perfecter of our faith" (Heb. 12:2) is not everywhere evident today. Indeed, Father Dulles laments, "The churches most involved in the ecumenical dialogues are often the least firm in their confessional witness."

This dilemma may well have been intensified ever since conscientious Catholic theologians, such as Father Dulles, have raised the ecumenical stakes considerably by currently teaching "what befits sound doctrine" (Tit. 2:1) since the providential promulgation of *Unitatis redintegratio* (1964). In face of these vigorous dogmatic challenges, many proponents of nondenominational rather than interconfessional approaches to church unity are now looking to greener pastures for their ecumenical "quick fix."[1]

There is a growing discernment that the triune God is at work in the great movements of secular history and the cataclysmic changes in non-Christian religious cultures. This, however, has led many to the indefensible conviction that we can become fellow workers with God only by leaving behind our ecclesiastical "ghetto" and working alongside persons of other faiths or of no faith so that we may do the things that God wants to have done in the world. It is therefore claimed that it is only in such groups of fellow servants of God that the real configurations of the true church will be found.

1. The following material is adapted from the author's lengthier analysis in "Evangelical Catholicity: Lutheran Identity in an Ecumenical Age," in Carl E. Braaten, ed., *The New Church Debate: Issues Facing American Lutheranism* (Philadelphia: Fortress, 1983), 15-38.

This has resulted in the growth of what is often called "secular ecumenism" or "catholic universalism," a widespread sense among conscientious persons of all races and creeds that the human family is one, and that everything that in practice denies this common humanity is an offense against God. Therefore many Christians now insist that the real task for our day is to manifest the unity of humankind rather than to realize the unity of the church. Nevertheless, the dialectical tension between church unity and world unity cannot and should not be eliminated. It can be properly maintained, however, only within the bounds of an authentic Christian eschatology.

In the course of recent ecumenical debates, a clearer distinction is increasingly being made between the universality of the world and the catholicity of the church. It underscores the fact that, within the tensions of an eschatological age, the search for the church's visible unity is to be understood as the quest for true catholicity—a catholicity that is continually received as a fresh gift of the Holy Spirit to a servant-church that is also, as is its divine head, willing to abandon its own life for the sake of its mission in and for the world. From the ways in which the term is loosely used today, however, one often gets the impression that "catholic" is simply a synonym of "universal" or "ecumenical." This only leads to doctrinal confusion, because these terms have an additional deeper or broader meaning alongside the common geographical one.

It must be recalled in this connection that the word *oikoumene* is the feminine passive participle of the verb *oikeo:* "to inhabit, dwell, reside" (in the intransitive) and "to occupy, to administer" (in the transitive). From the same verb come the nouns *oikia* or *oikos:* "house"; *oikema:* "habitation, construction, workshop"; and *paroikia:* "parish," with the idea of "living near" (the stress falling sometimes on the idea of having a neighbor, sometimes [as in the New Testament] on being a stranger to one's neighbors, whose political rights one does not share; hence, temporary residence abroad).

From this very rich etymology, therefore, we may infer that "ecumenism" bears a resemblance to the idea of a geographical dwelling, and moreover, to that of *provisional and fragile abode*. In Christian parlance, it refers to the eschatological reality that "here we have no lasting city" (Heb. 13:14).

Specifically, the word "ecumenical" comes from a Greek expression, *he oikoumene* (implying *ge* = earth), which means "the entire cultivated or inhabited world," as opposed to the desert. There is indisputably something universal, global in Christianity. And it is interesting to note in the history of the word itself this tendency to all-inclusiveness. Thus, for example, whereas in Matthew 24:14 "the whole world" means all the known universe and in Luke 2:1 the same word refers more precisely to the Roman Empire, the Revelation of John already uses the word in a more widely inclusive sense by opposing the policy of the kings or the field of awareness of "this world" to the policy of God or the field of awareness of the "world to come" (Rev. 3:10; 12:9; 16:14). And so with Basil of Caesarea, in the fourth century, it would seem the word *oikoumene,* which until then meant the whole of the Roman world and therefore of the known or "cultivated" world, came to mean the whole of the *inhabited* world, without regard to political frontiers, because Christian churches were to be found everywhere. The church catholic was thereby gradually detaching itself from the ecumenical empire.

I now risk carrying (doctrinal) coals to Newcastle as I distinguish "ecumenical" from "catholic." With regard to the term "catholic," the difference is that its original, fundamental meaning is a qualitative, eschatological one. The quantitative, geographical usage represents a later deviation, or still better, an application of the original meaning on a worldwide scale.

"Catholic" primarily signifies totality and wholeness, in the category of a doctrinal value judgment. It is used in the Christian era for describing the fullness of God's action in Christ, who then—and only then—reveals the truth to all persons, at all times, and in all places. That the early Christian writers respected this delicate distinction is also evident in the etymology of the Greek word *katolikos,* composed of *kata* and *olon* denoting a qualitative depth dimension. In the *Martyrdom of Polycarp* (8,1), for instance, we read ". . . of the catholic church which is throughout the *oikoumene (tes kata ten oikoumenen katolikes ekklesias)*." Here the church is clearly qualified as catholic, and only as such and because of this qualitative, unique, and distinctive property should it then be extended throughout the whole world.

These etymological remarks show why "catholic" refers primarily to the Christological essence of the church and only secondarily to its geographical extension. It reminds us of the biblical notion of fullness *(pleroma)* either in the sense that in Christ "the whole fulness of deity dwells bodily" (Col. 2:9); or that through the Spirit the faithful share in Christ, so that they may "know the love of Christ which surpasses knowledge, that you may be filled with all the fulness of God" (Eph. 3:19); or finally, that God has appointed Christ sovereign head of the church, which is truly Christ's body, the complement of him who fills all members with all grace (Eph. 1:22-23). In the Bible, "fullness" is applied first to the nature and action of God, in Christ, and only then it qualifies the nature of the body of Christ, the church, which is thus named "catholic" in order to designate its inner coherence with this unique, divine fullness.

Therefore we should not use "universal," "ecumenical," and "catholic" as sloppy synonyms. Nor should we speak redundantly of "secular ecumenism" or contradictorily of "catholic universalism," thereby confusing the church and the world, the new aeon and the old cosmos. We should first make the necessary distinction that the church is catholic as an eschatological reality, *before* the church addresses its message to the universal world or enters into critical solidarity with it. Only in this way can we remain faithful to the uniqueness of God's mighty act in Christ and to the unity and mission of Christ's holy body, the church catholic.

Furthermore, only through the unique acts and gifts of the Holy Spirit do we have the possibility of sharing in the lordship of Christ. The apostolic claim—that the good news of God springs from a particular set of events, a particular collection of documents, but that it is also of universal significance,

addresses a universal audience, and seeks a universal allegiance—has always been and continues to be an incarnational
scandal, a Messianic stumbling block, a Christological offense
(1 Cor. 1:23).

Our common calling today is to continue to make the
authentic apostolic witness that Christ-centered unity and mission are inseparable and must always be viewed dialectically in
the light of God's mercy and judgment. While all persons are
sinners before a righteous God, not all persons are victims in an
unjust society. This means that we must clearly distinguish
between the church and the world without falsely identifying
or separating the two. Our Christian hope lies neither in the
secularization of the church nor in the sacralization of the world.
Rather the church's worldly posture must remain in eschatological tension: nonpartisan in faith as it serves all sinful persons
alike in its ministry of word and sacrament; but then also
partisan in love as it struggles on behalf of the poor and the
oppressed in its ministry of mercy and justice.

The modern (misnamed) ecumenical movement affirms,
at its best, the inseparability of unity and mission within the
church catholic. This dual commitment is grounded in Christ's
revelation of God. Having prayed "that they may all be one,"
Christ immediately added, "so that the world may believe."
Christians are eschatologically called to participate in the eternal unity that the Son shares with the Father. They are thereby
incorporated into God's historical mission: sent into the world
by the Son, just as the Son was sent into that same world by the
Father (John 17:21; 20:21).

By way of conclusion, may I suggest respectfully that it
may well be the special calling of the Roman Catholic Church
today to help save the so-called ecumenical movement from
itself. "Ecumenical" is really a secular category; "catholic" is the
sacred one. (Today the United Nations is the most ecumenical
body on earth, but it can never become Catholic!)

What makes the church "catholic"—along with being one,
holy, and apostolic—is not merely that it is geographically
universal in breadth, but that it is universally orthodox in depth:

"that which has been believed and taught everywhere *(ubique)*, always *(semper)*, and by all *(ab omnibus)*," as defended by St. Vincent of Lerins and kindred catholic spirits both before and since. This declaration of trinitarian faith is grounded in the fullness of the church's universality, antiquity, and consensus in affirming the unique person and mission of our Lord Jesus: "I thank thee, Father, Lord of heaven and earth, that thou hast hidden these things from the wise and understanding and revealed them to babes; yea, Father, for such was thy gracious will. All things have been delivered to me by my Father; and no one knows the Son except the Father; and no one knows the Father except the Son and any one to whom the Son chooses to reveal him" (Matt. 11:25-27).

Since this is uniquely the promise of the gospel, only eschatological catholicity can save ecumenism from settling for geographical universality as the alleged grounds for visible church unity in full communion. Properly understood, therefore, I can only applaud the good judgment of Father Dulles in concluding with the profound counsel of Father Congar, "I believe more than ever that the essential ecumenical activity of the Catholic Church should be to live its own life more fully and genuinely."

Moreover, *Lumen gentium* subsequently acknowledged at Vatican Council II that "many elements of sanctification and truth" can be found outside the visible structure of the Catholic Church within which the *una sancta* "subsists," thus explicitly distancing itself from the institutional identification of the Mystical Body of Christ with the Roman Catholic Church, as clearly taught earlier by Pope Pius XII. Existing schisms mar the full manifestation of catholicity within any extant church body. You will therefore understand why at least this "separated brother" in Christ continues to pray and work for the fuller realization of those elements of catholicity which the council fathers also hopefully affirmed as "possessing an inner dynamism toward Christian unity." And if all this can continue to be done in patience and fidelity to the glory of God in the company of such gentle spirits as Avery Dulles, I will consider myself richly blessed.

Reflections on the Decree on Ecumenism: A Free Church Perspective

David T. Shannon

Introduction

My mind was challenged and my spirit warmed as I read the Decree on Ecumenism. I resonated with the affirmation that Christian unity was a major concern of the Roman Catholic Church. I concurred with its recognition of the scandal of disunity and felt I too could heed the call to join with those who longed for unity. In it I saw the Roman Catholic Church responding to the work of the Holy Spirit. Here it *recognized, acknowledged,* and *celebrated* the unity of the Christian church and joined the ecumenical movement. After reading the final sentence of the introduction, I felt it clear that the decree's primary audience was Roman Catholics. Here was their church's commitment to work for the restoration of unity among *all* followers of Christ (1).

David T. Shannon is Dean of the Interdenominational Theological Center in Atlanta, a member of both the World and National Council of Churches' Commissions on Faith and Order, and a member of International Baptist-Roman Catholic Conversation.

For me as a member of the Free Church tradition, this experience was like that of the person who overhears another's conversation. The language, style, and tone were different but not difficult to comprehend. Here I wish to state what I overheard and to share its implications as I see them. Then I shall share my five-year experience as a participant in the Roman Catholic-Baptist International Conversation.

The Decree

The language of the decree is theological, sacramental, ethical, and eschatological. It begins by calling all to recognize God's revelation in Jesus Christ. This sets the tone of the document, which is a theological affirmation grounded in Christ's prayer for the unity of the church (John 17:21). At the same time it is sacramental because it proclaims: "In his Church [Christ] instituted the wonderful sacrament of the Eucharist by which the unity of the Church is both signified and brought about." It further affirms that the call to unity is founded on the commandment to love one another. Finally the Holy Spirit is viewed as "their Advocate, who, as Lord and life-giver, should remain with them forever" (2).

According to the decree, unity is a fact:

> The Church, then, God's only flock like a standard lifted on high for the nations to see it, ministers the Gospel of peace to all mankind, as it makes its pilgrim way in hope toward its goal, the fatherland above.
>
> This is the sacred mystery of the unity of the Church, in Christ and through Christ, with the Holy Spirit energizing its various functions. The highest exemplar and source of this mystery is the unity, in the Trinity of Persons, of one God, the Father and the Son in the Holy Spirit.

It then notes the divisions and the rifts that do exist among Christians. Its style is triumphal, yet conciliatory. It says that people who believe in Christ and have been truly baptized are in communion with the Catholic Church, even though this communion is imperfect. Finally Catholics are challenged not only to recognize the action of God in the ecumenical movement but also to become participants.

The second chapter sets forth principles for active participation in the ecumenical movement, beginning with a call to repentance. This is followed by an exhortation to live "spiritual ecumenism," or public and private prayer for unity and witnessing to unity already achieved. The decree proposes theological study and dialogue, as well as proper ministerial formation marked by ecumenical sensitivity. It then gives special attention to the principles of dialogue in which theologians are told to stand firm in the teaching of the Church, but to proceed with love for the truth, with charity, and with humility.

The practice of ecumenism is seen both as a confession of the triune God and as a Christian witness to the world. The decree affirms that through study and mutual cooperation believers can get to know each other better and so pave the way for Christian unity. It also discusses those churches and ecclesial communities that are separated from the Roman Apostolic See. This is followed by a clear exposition of some of the issues involved in the quest for Christian unity, including: (1) confessing Jesus as God and Lord, the sole mediator between God and men and women; (2) the relationship between Scripture and church; (3) the sacrament of baptism; (4) the Lord's Supper; (5) and the application of the gospel to moral conduct. The decree concludes with a call for the faithful to refrain from "frivolous or imprudent zeal" and to act in such a way that no obstacle be put in the way to Christian unity.

From my Free Church tradition, I note five positive points in the decree:

1. It calls on all Roman Catholics to engage in the movement toward ecumenical unity.
2. It affirms ecumenism's theological, biblical, and historical bases.

3. It clearly sets forth the need for repentance and openness.
4. It stresses the need for study, dialogue, and mutual cooperation.
5. It challenges Catholics to become advocates for ecumenism.

But I would also make five negative observations:

1. The decree suffers from what has been called the "language bubble," that is, it often uses triumphal language.
2. It does not recognize the full range of Christian churches, such as the Coptic and the Armenian. There seems to be a pro-Western bias.
3. It does not stress praxis, but calls for unity in doctrine and sacraments.
4. It does not identify processes for interchurch interaction except through dialogue and mutual cooperation in social action.
5. It places more emphasis on ecclesiology than on ethical issues such as love, peace, and justice, which are components of an authentic ecumenism.

During the last five years I participated in the International Conversations between the Roman Catholic Church and the World Baptist Alliance. Our topic was "Christian Witness in Today's World"; our goal was to come to a mutual understanding of certain issues upon which we felt convergence or divergence. Other goals included maintaining channels of communication for mutual as well as self-understanding; identifying new avenues for common witness; and addressing those prejudices that exist between our two world confessional families.

The participants at each session presented scholarly papers, shared in Bible studies related to our themes, and visited local communities. We had five such "conversations" and reached remarkable consensus on many issues. Significant differences remain, however, indicating the need for further dialogues.[1] In summary form here is what we could proclaim together:

Witness to Christ

Our common witness rests on shared faith in the centrality of Jesus Christ as the revelation of God and the sole mediator between God and humankind (1 Tim. 2:5). We come to know Jesus Christ through the Scriptures, especially the New Testament, which we share in common as the source and sustainer of our faith. That knowledge is experientially confirmed by the internal witness of the Holy Spirit, is handed down by the community of believers, and is certified by the authoritative witness of the church throughout the ages. We are also aware that God set forth in Christ "the mystery of his will" (Eph. 1:9).

The distinction between the person and the work of Christ, while helpful to later theology, does not capture the riches of the biblical testimony to Jesus Christ. The christological statements in the New Testament express the faith of individuals and groups. In their earliest forms such as we find in Paul's resurrection *paradosis* (1 Cor. 15:1-11) and in the "kerygmatic" speeches of Acts (e.g., 2:22-24; 3:14-16; 4:10-12; 10:40-43), Jesus is proclaimed as the one whom God raised up (or made Lord and Messiah) for our sins or in whose name we are saved. The doctrine of the person of Christ cannot be separated from the message of the saving work that God accomplished in and through Christ.

1. We first met in West Berlin (July 18-21, 1984) and focused on "Evangelism/Evangelization: The Mission of the Church." Our second session assembled in Los Angeles (June 24-30, 1985) and addressed the issues "Christology" and "Conversion/Discipleship" as aspects of "Witness to Christ." The third convention convened in New York City (June 2-7, 1986) and explored "The Church as Koinonia of the Spirit." The fourth, in Rome (July 13-18, 1987), directed itself to specific issues standing in the way of common Christian witness, namely, proselytism and restrictions on religious freedom. The fifth was held in Atlanta (July 18-23, 1988) and sought to assess the entire series.

The New Testament speaks of Jesus in different ways. The Synoptic Gospels present Jesus as the one who proclaims the advent of God's reign and enacts it in his ministry (Mark 1:14-15). He calls sinners to repentance (Luke 4:16-19). He gathers disciples who were to be with him and to be sent by him (Mark 3:13-15). He possesses a unique familiarity with God and teaches those who follow him to pray to God as Father (Matt. 6:7-15) and to walk in loving trust in God's power and presence (Matt. 6:25-33). He summons those who would follow him to love God and neighbor with their whole heart, mind, and soul (Mark 12:28-34) and gives his life as a ransom that others may be free (Mark 10:45).

The Gospel of John is a rich source of understanding Christ, and its language and perspective gave shape to the christological formulation of the councils. It was written in order that people might believe that Jesus was the Christ, the Son of God, and that believing they might have life in his name (John 20:31). Jesus is presented as the Word who was with God from the beginning and through whom all things were made (John 1:1-3). This Word became flesh and dwelt among us so that his glory could be seen. He was full of grace and truth (John 1:14). Eternal life was to know the one true God and Jesus Christ whom God had sent (John 17:3). Access to this eternal life was by way of faith. The Christian was summoned to confess with Martha, "Lord, I believe that you are the Christ, the Son of God, he who is coming into the world" (John 11:27). Through the death and resurrection of Jesus the Holy Spirit was given for the remission of sin (John 20:22-23). Through the witness of the Paraclete the disciples were made witnesses to Christ (John 15:26-27). Jesus in dying prayed for them that the Father keep them in his name and make them one (John 17:11).

Jesus is proclaimed as the one descended from David according to the flesh and is designated Son of God in power according to the Spirit of holiness by his resurrection from the dead (Rom. 1:4). He is also the suffering servant and the Son of Man who came not to be served but to serve (Mark 10:45). He is the Savior born for us in the city of David (Luke 2:11) and the one who, though equal to God, emptied himself, taking on the form of a servant, being born in human likeness (Phil. 2:7).

The work of Christ is presented under a variety of metaphors such as justification (Gal. 2:16; Rom. 3:26-28; 5:18), salvation (2 Cor. 7:10; Rom. 1:16; 10:10; 13:11), expiation and redemption (Rom. 3:24-25; 8:32), and reconciliation (2 Cor. 5:18-20; Rom. 5:10-11). These expressions point to the ontological, objective event wherein God has begun the restoration of a fallen humanity to relationship with himself and has inaugurated a renewal of creation through Christ's death on the cross and resurrection from the dead. The offer of salvation from God in Christ is received in faith, which is a gift of God "who desires all people to be saved and to come to the knowledge of the truth" (1 Tim. 2:4).

Conclusions concerning Witness

Discussion of our witness to Christ has revealed that our two communions are one in their confession of Jesus Christ as Son of God, Lord and Savior. The faith in Christ proclaimed in the New Testament and expressed in the first four ecumenical councils is shared by both of our churches. Our discussion uncovered no significant differences with regard to the doctrine of the person and work of Christ, although some did appear with regard to the appropriation of Christ's saving work. We believe that this communion of faith in Christ should be stressed and rejoiced in as a basis for our discussion of other areas of church doctrine and life, where serious differences may remain.

While affirming that the Scriptures are our primary source for the revelation of God in Jesus, we give different weight to creeds and confessional statements. Roman Catholics affirm that sacred Scripture and sacred tradition flow "from the same divine well-spring" and that "the Church does not draw her certainty about all revealed truths from the holy Scriptures alone" (Dogmatic Constitution on Divine Revelation, 9). The faith of the church expressed in its creeds through the ages is normative for Catholics. Baptists, while affirming the creeds of the first four ecumenical councils and producing confessional statements in their history, do not hold them as normative for the individual believer or for subsequent periods of church life. For Baptists, the Scriptures alone are normative, although confessional statements are sometimes useful in highlighting biblical emphases.

Conversion

Together we affirm that Jesus inaugurated his public ministry by announcing the advent of God's reign and by summoning people to be converted and to believe in the gospel (Mark 1:14-15). He immediately summoned disciples to follow him (Mark 1:16-20). Saul, the persecutor of the early Christians, through a revelation of the gospel of Jesus becomes Paul the apostle to the Gentiles (Gal. 2:1-10). The mystery of who Jesus is and what he did for us can ultimately be grasped only in faith and in the practice of Christian discipleship through hope and love (1 Thess. 1:3).

After his resurrection Jesus announced to his disciples that "repentance and forgiveness of sins should be preached in his name to all nations" (Luke 24:47). Before he departed from his disciples Jesus commissioned them to make disciples of all nations, baptizing them and teaching them to observe all that he commanded them (Matt. 28:16-20). After Pentecost the disciples began to proclaim repentance and forgiveness of sins to all nations (Acts 2:5-13). Under the guidance of the same Spirit that was given to the disciples at Pentecost, in its preaching and witness the church strives to fulfill the mandate of Jesus and through the ages renews this proclamation of conversion and forgiveness.

Conversion is turning away from all that is opposed to God, contrary to Christ's teaching, and turning to God, to

Christ, the Son, through the work of the Holy Spirit. It entails a turning from the self-centeredness of sin to faith in Christ as Lord and savior. Conversion is a passing from one way of life to another new one, marked with the newness of Christ. It is a continuing process so that the whole life of a Christian should be a passage from death to life, from error to truth, from sin to grace. Our life in Christ demands continual growth in God's grace. Conversion is personal but not private. Individuals respond in faith to God's call, but faith comes from hearing the proclamation of the word of God and is to be expressed in the life together in Christ that is the church.

Conversion and discipleship are related to one another as birth to life. Conversion is manifested in a life of discipleship. In the Gospels Jesus summoned disciples to be with him and to share his ministry of proclaiming the advent of God's reign and bringing the healing power of this reign into human life. He also summoned them to be like him in taking up their crosses and in living in loving service to others. After Easter and Pentecost the early community continued to announce and spread the good news and to witness to the saving power of God. Like Jesus, the disciples were persecuted, but through the gift of the Spirit they remained faithful and continued to proclaim the gospel.

Throughout history God continues to summon people to follow Jesus, and by the gift of the Spirit and the power of faith the risen Lord continues his ministry. Discipleship consists in personal attachment to Jesus and in commitment to proclamation of the gospel and to those actions that bring the healing and saving power of Jesus to men and women today. The disciple is nurtured by the Scriptures, worship, prayer in all its forms, works of mercy toward others, proclamation, instruction, and the witness of daily life. The church, which can be called a community of disciples, is gathered in the name and presence of the risen Christ. This community is summoned to share the gift it has received. The gift is thus a mandate for a tireless effort to call all people to repentance and faith. A community of disciples of Jesus is always a community in mission.

Conclusions concerning Conversion

As Baptists and Catholics we both strive to be converted and believe in the good news (Mark 1:14). Yet, conversion and discipleship are expressed differently in our ecclesial communions. Baptists stress the importance of an initial experience of personal conversion wherein the believer accepts the gift of God's saving and assuring grace. Baptism and entry into the church are testimony to this gift, which is expressed in a life of faithful discipleship. For Catholics baptism is the sacrament by which a person is incorporated into Christ and is reborn so as to share in the divine life. It is always consequent upon faith; in the case of an infant, this faith is considered to be supplied by the community. Catholics speak of the need for a life of continual conversion expressed in the sacrament of reconciliation (penance), which in the early church was sometimes called a "second baptism." In both of our communions changes in church practice challenge us to consider more deeply our theology of conversion and baptism. In the recently instituted "Rite for the Christian Initiation of Adults," Roman Catholics affirm that the baptism of adults is the paradigm for a full understanding of baptism. On the other hand, in some areas of the world Baptists receive baptism at a very early age.

The Church

Our discussions on the church centered on the "*Koinonia* of the Spirit" (Phil. 2:1; cf. 2 Cor. 13:14) because it is a helpful description of our common understanding of the church. *Koinonia* suggests more than is implied by the English terms used to translate it, such as "fellowship" or "community." Based on the root idea of "sharing in one reality held in common," it was used in a variety of ways by the early Christians. According to 1 Cor. 1:9, Christians are "called into the fellowship of his Son," which means the same as being "in Christ" or being a member of the

Body of Christ (1 Cor. 12:12ff.). As we participate in Christ, we participate in the gospel (1 Cor. 9:23; Phil. 1:5), in faith (Philem. 5), and in the Lord's Supper (1 Cor. 10:16ff.). To share in the Supper is to share in Christ's body and blood (v. 16). Fellowship with Christ entails participation in his life (Rom. 6:8; 2 Cor. 7:3), sufferings (Rom. 8:17; 2 Cor. 7:3; Gal. 2:19-20), resurrection (Col. 2:12; 3:1; Eph. 2:6), and eternal reign (Rom. 8:17; 2 Tim. 2:12). For Paul *koinonia* with the risen Christ is the same as *koinonia* with the Spirit (2 Cor. 13:14) and with other Christians. This is more than a bond of friendship. All share in the spiritual blessings of the Spirit and are thus obligated to help one another (Rom. 12:13) in their afflictions (Phil. 4:14) as well as in their blessings. In 1 John to be a Christian means to have *koinonia* with God, Father and Son (1:3, 6)—and with other believers (1:3, 7). The accent is placed on active participation—"walking and doing"—as an expression of this fellowship.

Discussion of the passages cited above led to the following conclusions: (1) that in and through Christ God has laid down the foundation of the church; (2) that *koinonia* both between God and human beings and within the church is a divine gift; and (3) that the Spirit effects the continuity between the church and Jesus. The uniting of a diverse humanity—Jews and Greeks, males and females, slaves and masters (Gal. 3:28)—in one body could not have occurred on human initiative. It depended, rather, on God's action through Jesus Christ—dead, buried, and risen. We are now called into communion with God and with one another in the Risen One. God actually binds us together in an intimate fellowship through the Holy Spirit. God offers the Spirit as a gift to the whole community of faith to guide it and nurture it and bring it to maturity.

Koinonia, whether between God and humanity or among human beings, must be regarded as a gift of God. Though made "in the image of God," both male and female (Gen. 1:27), to dwell in community, Adam, humanity, has ruptured the relationship with God and with one another that would make such community possible. God's long-suffering love alone sufficed to salvage a broken humanity, through Israel and, above all, through God's Son, Jesus Christ, the new Adam. In the Son God did for us what we could not do for ourselves. The free gift of God in Christ surpassed by far the effects of Adam's transgression (Rom. 5:15-17).

The Spirit continues in the church the redemptive work God began in the Son. In baptism the Spirit unites the diverse members—Jew and Gentile, slave and freeborn, male and female, and, we could add, black and white, rich and poor, etc.—into a single body (1 Cor. 12:12-13; Gal. 3:28). The Spirit is the ground of every dimension of the church's life—worship, interior growth, witness to an unbelieving world, and proclamation of the gospel (Acts 2:42-47; 4:32-37). The Spirit apportions different "gifts" with which the members may build up the body of Christ and carry out the mission of the church (1 Cor. 12:4-11, 27-30; Rom. 12:4-8).

Conclusions concerning the Church

Koinonia, which is at the heart of the church, is the result of the manifold activity of the Spirit. In the church there are varieties of gifts but the same Spirit, varieties of service but the same Lord, and varieties of working but the same God, and, though composed of many members, the church is the one body of Christ (1 Cor. 12:4; Rom. 12:5). When Baptists speak of "church" they refer primarily to the local congregation gathered by the Spirit in obedience and service to God's word. Catholics by "church" refer to the community of faith, hope, and charity as a visible structure established and sustained on earth by Christ (Dogmatic Constitution on the Church, 8). While both Baptists and Catholics admit the presence of Christ in the church (Matt. 18:20; 28:20), they understand this in different ways. Catholics believe that the church is a "society structured with hierarchical organs and the mystical body of Christ [that] are not to be thought of as two realities. On the contrary, they form one complex reality which comes together from a human and a divine element" (ibid.). Baptists affirm that the church is divine as to its origin, mission, and scope, and human as to its historical existence and structure.

Evangelism/Evangelization

The gift of faith we have received is a gift to be shared with others. Jesus was sent by God to proclaim the good news of God (Mark 1:14; cf. Luke 4:18; 7:22). He sent the Twelve (Matt. 10:5ff.) and the Seventy (Luke 10:1ff.) to carry the same message. After the resurrection he directed his followers to go into all the world and make disciples (Matt. 28:16-20) and commissioned them to be witnesses to the ends of the earth (Acts 1:8). The church has engaged in this task throughout its history.

Both Baptists and Roman Catholics respond to this summons through a ministry of evangelism or evangelization. Baptists typically emphasize free personal response of individuals to the gospel, often to the neglect of corporate responsibility. In more recent years, however, some Baptist groups have focused less on individuals and more on the corporate and social implications of evangelism/evangelization. (Some Baptist groups have tried to match an emphasis on the individual with attention to the corporate and social implications of evangelism/evangelization.)

Roman Catholics apply the term "evangelization" to the "first proclamation" of the gospel to nonbelievers (Apostolic Exhortation on Evangelization, 21) and also in the wider sense of the renewal of humanity, witness, inner adherence, entry into the community, acceptance of signs, and apostolic initiative. These elements are complementary and mutually enriching (ibid., 24). Christ is the center and end of missionary effort. Catholic emphasis upon incarnation, however, encourages a greater concern for "inculturation" than does Baptist emphasis upon redemption of fallen humanity from sin. It also opens the way for assigning sacraments a more prominent place in the evangelization task.

Recent ecumenical developments have led to increased appreciation by Roman Catholics and Baptists for each other and for other Christian bodies and may open the way to common witness. Several documents of the Second Vatican Council, along with later documents, speak of many factors uniting Catholics and Protestants: faith, baptism, sharing in the life of grace, union in the Holy Spirit, the Christian life, and discipleship. While Vatican II maintained that the church of Christ, "constituted and organized as a society in the present world, subsists in the Catholic Church" (Dogmatic Constitution on the Church, 8), it also acknowledged that "some, even very many, of the most significant elements or endowments which together go to build up and give life to the Church itself, can exist outside the visible boundaries of the Catholic Church" (Decree on Ecumenism, 3).

Non-Christian Religions

Baptists and Roman Catholics differ among themselves about salvation within non-Christian religions. The Second Vatican Council brought to an end the negative attitude toward them that had prevailed in the church and made it possible to enter into dialogue with them about some of the common problems of the present that need global attention. The council expressed its high regard for the manner of life, precept, and doctrines of these religions, which "often reflect a ray of that truth which enlightens all men" (Declaration on the Relationship of the Church to Non-Christian Religions, 2). At the same time the council made it clear that the church "proclaims and is in duty bound to proclaim without fail, Christ who is the way, the truth, and the life (John 14:6). In him, in whom "God reconciled all things to himself (2 Cor. 5:18-19), men find the fulness of their religious life" (ibid.). Baptists have issued no major statements on salvation through other religions, but most construe the biblical pronouncement that "there is no other name under heaven given among humankind by which we must be saved"

(Acts 4:12) in a rather strict fashion. They frequently cite also "I am the way, and the truth, and the life; no one comes to the Father, but by me" (John 14:6) and apply it in the narrow sense. Some Baptists, nevertheless, have engaged in dialogue or conversations with representatives of the other major world religions. Similarly, they discern the need for cooperation among world religions to solve urgent human problems.

Challenges to Common Witness

We respond to the summons to be heralds of the good news by proclaiming the name of Jesus to humankind in such a manner that people will be led to believe in Jesus Christ and to live as true Christians. As we strive to make our lives a witness of the faith that sustains us, certain issues emerge that are of common concern.

An important area of common concern is the language we use in speaking of our common witness. "Common witness" means that Christians, even though not yet in full communion with one another, bear witness together to many vital aspects of Christian truth and Christian life. We affirm that it embraces the whole of life: divine worship, responsible service, proclamation of the good news with a view to leading men and women, under the power of the Holy Spirit, to salvation and gathering them into the body of Christ.

Realizing that "for freedom Christ has set us free" (Gal. 5:1), we seek ways that people may respond to the gospel in freedom and love. We also confess that competition and bitterness among Christian missionaries have often been a stumbling block for those to whom we seek to proclaim the gospel. Often Christian missionaries are accused of "proselytism," which in both secular and religious circles has taken on the pejorative connotation of the use of methods that compromise rather than enhance the freedom of the believer and of the gospel.

A historical overview shows that the understanding of "proselytism" has changed considerably. In the Bible it was devoid of negative connotations. A "proselyte" was someone who, by belief in Yahweh and acceptance of the law, became a member of the Jewish community. Christianity took over this meaning to describe a person who converted from paganism. Mission work and proselytism were considered equivalent concepts until recent times.

More recently the term "proselytism" in its pejorative sense has come to be applied by some to the attempts of various Christian confessions to win members *from each other.* This raises the delicate question regarding the difference between evangelism/evangelization and proselytism.

As Baptists and Catholics we agree that evangelization is a primary task of the church and that every Christian has the right and obligation to share and spread the faith. We also agree that faith is the free response by which people, empowered by the grace of God, commit themselves to the gospel of Christ. It is contrary to the message of Christ, to the ways of God's grace, and to the personal character of faith that any means be used that would reduce or impede the freedom of a person to make a basic Christian comment.

We believe that there are certain marks that should characterize the witness we bear in the world. We affirm:

- that witness must be given in a spirit of love and humility;
- that it leaves the addressee full freedom to make a personal decision;
- that it does not prevent either individuals or communities from bearing witness to their own convictions, including religious ones.

We also admit that there are negative aspects of witness that should be avoided, and we acknowledge in a spirit of repentance that both of us have been guilty of proselytism in its negative sense. We affirm that the following things should be avoided:

- every kind of physical violence, moral compulsion, and psychological pressure (for example, we noted the use of certain advertising techniques in mass media that might bring undue pressure on readers/viewers);

- explicit or implicit offers of temporal or material advantages such as prizes for changing one's religious allegiance;
- improper use of situations of distress, weakness, or lack of education to bring about conversion;
- using political, social, and economic pressure as a means of obtaining conversion or hindering others, especially minorities, in the exercise of their religious freedom;
- casting unjust and uncharitable suspicion on other denominations;
- comparing the strengths and ideals of one community with the weaknesses and practices of another community.

On the basis of this understanding of proselytism, we agree that the freedom of the gospel and the individual must be respected in any process of evangelism/evangelization. We are aware, however, that often the charge of "proselytism" in a negative sense can be made when one communion comes in contact with the evangelism/evangelization of the other. Every effort must be made to increase mutual knowledge and understanding and to respect the integrity and rights of other individuals and communities to live and proclaim the gospel according to their own traditions and convictions. In an increasingly secularized world, division and religious strife between Christian bodies can be such a scandal that nonbelievers may not be attracted to the gospel.

Religious Liberty

From the time of Constantine until the modern period, the Christian church has experienced a wide variety of relationships to secular authority where, by custom, law, and concordat, civil authority and the church have been intertwined in many areas of life. Unfortunately, these interrelationships have sometimes

led to intolerance and consequent suffering. In some traditionally Roman Catholic countries, Baptists were sometimes deprived of their full civil and religious rights and freedom. On the
other hand, in areas where Baptists were a numerical majority
or enjoyed greater economic or social power, Roman Catholics,
although supposedly enjoying all civil rights, sometimes suffered
discrimination, injustice, and intolerance.

Baptists were among the first to advocate the separation
of church and state. Having been formed in an age of religious
strife and persecution, Baptists have historically advocated freedom of conscience and practice in religious matters, not simply
for Baptists but for all persons.

Historically Roman Catholics and Baptists have differed
over the relation of the church to civil authority and on the
question of religious liberty. With the Declaration on Religious
Liberty of the Second Vatican Council, Roman Catholicism
affirmed strongly that "the human person has a right to religious freedom" (2) and that this freedom means that all men
and women "should be immune from coercion on the part of
individuals, social groups and every human power so that,
within due limits, nobody is forced to act against his convictions . . . in religious matters" (ibid.). The council states that this
freedom "is based on the very dignity of the human person as
known through the revealed Word of God and by reason itself "
(ibid.). Since religious liberty is a right that flows from the
dignity of the person, civil authorities have an obligation to
respect and protect this right.

Both Baptists and Catholics agree that religious freedom
is rooted in the New Testament. Jesus proclaimed God's reign
and summoned people to a deep personal conversion (Mark
1:14-15) that demands that a person be able to respond freely
to God's offer of grace. The apostle Paul resisted all those who
attempted to coerce the churches into practices or beliefs that
he felt contrary to the freedom won by the death and resurrection of Christ.

In the area of religious freedom Roman Catholics and
Baptists can fruitfully explore different forms of common wit-

ness. Both groups struggle to exist in situations where religious freedom is not respected. Both are concerned about those who suffer persecution because of their faith.

In certain traditionally Roman Catholic countries civil constitutions and laws enacted prior to the Second Vatican Council have not been changed to reflect the teaching of the council. In some settings with a dominant Baptist majority the traditional Baptist stress on separation of church and state as a means to assure religious freedom has been weakened. Both groups need to exercise greater vigilance to ensure respect for religious liberty.

Christians have a right and a duty to bring their religious insights and values to the public debate about the structure and direction of a society. This may also include the effort to embody their values in civil law. As they do so, however, they should always be sensitive to and considerate of the rights of individual conscience and of minorities and of the welfare of the society as a whole. They should measure their efforts against Jesus' command to love one's neighbor as oneself, his proclamation that both the just and the unjust have the same loving Father, and his own concern for marginal groups in his society.

Theological Authority and Method

These Baptist-Roman Catholic conversations frequently uncovered different views on theological authority and method. The theoretical reason for that is clear: Baptists rely on the Scriptures alone, as interpreted under the guidance of the Holy Spirit, the Reformation principle. Roman Catholics receive God's revelation from the Scriptures interpreted in the light of tradition, under the leadership of the magisterium, in a communal process guided by the Holy Spirit. We found that these differences are not as sharp as this formulation would suggest. At the Second Vatican Council the Roman Catholic Church dealt carefully and in detail with the relationship between Scripture and tradition (Dogmatic Constitution on Divine Revelation, 2). It endeavored to reach and express an understanding of the relationship between Scripture, tradition, and the teaching office of the church (magisterium). Each of these has its own place in the presentation of the truth of Jesus Christ. The place of one is not identical with that of the other, yet in the Roman Catholic view these three combine together to present divine revelation. On the other hand, Baptists invoke the Baptist heritage as decisively as Roman Catholics cite tradition, usually disclaiming that it bears the same authority as Scripture but holding on to it vigorously nonetheless.

Roman Catholics often ask how Baptists regard the crucial theological statements that the church has issued in its walk through history, such as, for example, the great christological statements of Nicea and Constantinople. Baptists, looking at certain dogmas that they regard as grounded in tradition rather than in Scripture, for example, the immaculate conception and the assumption of Mary, ask whether Roman Catholics set any limits to what can be defined. Can the church simply approve anything it wants as official doctrine? The key issue needing discussion here is that of development of doctrine.

The Shape of *Koinonia*

Another issue that distinguishes our communions is the different ways in which the *koinonia* of the Spirit is made concrete. Baptists and Catholics obviously conceive of the Spirit working through different structures. For Baptists, *koinonia* is expressed principally in local congregations gathered voluntarily under the lordship of Jesus Christ for worship, fellowship, instruction, evangelism, and mission. In accordance with their heritage they recognize the Spirit's direction through the interdependency of associations, conventions, alliances, and other bodies designed to proclaim the good news and to carry out the world mission of Christ. However, they have sought to avoid developing structures that would threaten the freedom of individuals and the autonomy of local congregations. For Roman Catholics, the *koinonia* that the Spirit effects in the local congregation is simultaneously a *koinonia* with the other local congregations in the one universal church. Correspondingly, they recognize the Spirit's activity in the spiritual and institutional bonds that unite congregations into dioceses presided over by bishops and that unite dioceses into the whole church, presided over by the Bishop of Rome. Vital to future ecumenical progress would be further discussion of the relationship between the Spirit and ecclesiastical structures.

Relationship between Faith, Baptism, and Christian Witness

Our conversations revealed a growing common concern about the authenticity of faith, baptism, and Christian witness. Baptists, viewing faith primarily as the response of the individual to God's free gift of grace, insist that the faith response precedes baptism. Baptist congregations, however, vary in the way they receive persons baptized as infants in other congregations. Practices range from the rebaptism of all persons who have not received baptism at the hands of a Baptist minister to acceptance of all persons baptized by any mode, whether as infants or as adults (on confession of faith in Jesus Christ). Roman Catholics regard the sacraments, such as baptism, in a context of faith as an exercise of the power of the risen Christ, comparable to that exercised by Jesus when he cured the sick and freed the possessed. Emphasizing the corporate as well as the individual nature of faith, they baptize infants and catechize them through a process culminating in full participation in the church.

Both approaches present some difficulties. Baptists are not at one on how children relate to the church prior to baptism. Some churches now have "child dedication" rites, but most have not dealt with the issue at all. Baptist "rebaptism" (viewed by them as a first baptism) often offends Christians of other communions because it suggests that the others are not really Christian and because it seems to violate the scriptural call for "one baptism." Roman Catholics and others who practice infant baptism, on the other hand, confront the fact that there is little clear evidence in the Scriptures for this practice. The baptizing of infants thus seems to be sustained principally by tradition and a more corporate understanding of faith.

The heart of the problem to be addressed here seems to be the nature of faith and the nature of the sacraments (called "ordinances" by most Baptists) that raise a number of questions Baptists and Catholics must address together. Is faith solely an individual's response to God's gift? Can the faith of the community stand as the personal faith of an infant? May one speak of a "community of faith," that is, of the body of Christ as itself a subject with a common faith in which individual believers participate? Are the sacraments outward signs of a preceding inner commitment? Are they the means through which Christ himself effects his healing and saving work? What does it mean to say that baptism is "the sacrament of faith"? The issues between us are not likely to be resolved without addressing these questions.

Clarification of Key Terms

We are aware that religious tension between communities can arise from different understanding and use of similar terms. A fundamental concept in both our communions is that of "mission." In its most extensive sense Baptists speak of the mission of the church to glorify God by making him known through faith in Jesus Christ. Roman Catholics also speak of "mission" in its broadest sense as everything that the church does in service to the kingdom of God. Baptists understand mission, often spoken of as "missions" with reference to the many outward movements of the church, as the major means by which the church accomplishes its witness to the world.

Baptists almost never use the term "evangelization" but prefer the term "evangelism" to describe how believers, individually or collectively, take the gospel of Christ to the world, going everywhere preaching the word (Acts 8:4). "Evangelization" until recent years was not frequently used within Roman Catholicism. The best working definition can be found in the Apostolic Exhortation of Pope Paul VI, "On Evangelization in the Modern World" (1975), in which it is said to comprise three major activities: (1) *evangelism,* understood as the proclamation of the gospel to the unchurched within one's own society or culture; (2) *missionary activity,* which involves cross-cultural proclamation of the gospel; and (3) *pastoral activity*—nourishing and deepening the gospel among those already committed to it.

Even with a growing convergence in terminology, evangelism/evangelization assumes different forms within our two communions. The Baptist stress on conversion as an act of personal faith and acceptance of Jesus as Lord and savior gives precedence to leading people to an explicit confession of faith through proclamation of the gospel. Roman Catholics stress that by baptism a person is made new in Christ in the church and stress the establishment of a Christian community through proclamation of the word and through a ministry of presence and service.

Within these different emphases, however, there are strong similarities. Both communions stress the need for unbelievers and the unchurched to hear and live the message of salvation expressed in the Scriptures, and both strive to fulfill Jesus' command to love the neighbor by engaging in works of mercy and charity both at home and in "mission" countries.

Mary in Faith and Practice

Devotion to Mary has traditionally been an area of great difference between Roman Catholics and Baptists. It also emerged in our discussions as a challenge to common witness. Baptists in general have two major problems with Marian devotion: (1) it seems to compromise the sole mediatorship of Jesus as Lord and savior; and (2) Marian doctrines such as the immaculate conception and the assumption that Catholics proclaim as infallible and hence to be believed in faith seem to have little explicit grounding in the Bible. According to Roman Catholics, devotion to Mary does not compromise the unique role of Christ, is rooted in her intimate relationship to Jesus, reflects her continuing role in salvation history, and has a solid basis in the New Testament.

Because of the long history of misunderstanding and the theological difficulties and subtleties inherent in Marian doctrines, we do not expect consensus in the foreseeable future. In an area such as devotion to Mary, which evokes both strong emotions and strong convictions from both communions, the quest for mutual understanding and respect is put to the test. Roman Catholics must attempt to understand and sympathize with the serious problems Baptists have with Marian devotion and doctrine. Baptists must try to understand not only the biblical and the theological grounds of Marian doctrine and devotion, but its significance in popular piety and religious practice.

Ways to Common Witness

Conversations between Baptists and Roman Catholics will not lead in the near future to full communion between our two bodies. This fact, however, should not prevent the framing of concrete ways to witness together at the present time. It will be helpful to think of several different levels—international, national, regional, and local—in which Catholics and Baptists could speak or act in concert. Such cooperation is already taking place in a variety of ways: translation of the Scriptures into indigenous languages, theological education, common concern and shared help in confronting famine and other natural disasters, health care for the underprivileged, advocacy of human rights and religious liberty, working for peace and justice, and strengthening of the family. Baptists and Catholics could enhance their common witness by speaking and acting together more in these and other areas. A whole row of issues vital to the survival of humankind lies before us.

Conclusions

My study of the Decree on Ecumenism and my participation in the Roman Catholic-Baptist International Conversations lead me to make the following observations. Ecumenism is a fact of our time for Roman Catholics.[2] It equally manifests the commitment of other Christians, too. But more than that, we can note a shift in focus from differences to the recognition, acknowledgment, and celebration of the unity that we already have as one body in Christ. For us in the Free Church tradition it is a great consolation to know that the primacy of Scripture

---

2. Robert S. Bilheimer in his recent book, *Breakthrough: The Emergence of the Ecumenical Tradition* (Grand Rapids: Eerdmans, 1989), indicates the significance of the Roman Catholic Church in the ecumenical movement. "Frequently, this idea of *vestigia ecclesiae* had been used negatively, in the sense of 'only traces.' Toronto turned the idea around and made it the basis of dialogue. 'Traces,' in ecumenical usage, do not call forth condescension, but are welcomed as 'hopeful signs pointing toward real unity'" (53). "On at least one occasion Roman Catholics helped the WCC substantially and perhaps decisively. In 1949, a year before the Toronto Statement was worked out, ten Roman Catholics and ten WCC people met at the Istina Center in Paris. Father Yves Congar, whom Visser 't Hooft called 'the father of Roman Catholic ecumenism,' strongly suggested that the concept of *vestigia ecclesiae* yielded a sound starting point for ecumenical eccesiology; and Father Jean Daniélou urged that 'a dynamic understanding of *vestigia ecclesiae* be worked out.' That concept was indeed to play a major role at Toronto. Visser 't Hooft obviously felt himself bound to secrecy concerning this germinal meeting until well after Vatican II. Closely as we discussed matters, he never mentioned it, nor did rumor of it come from the other nine. All had clearly agreed to keep silence for the sake of the Roman Catholic pioneers" (107).

and freedom of conscience are affirmed and underscored by all. The Decree on Ecumenism has been a powerful force in enabling our churches to arrive at this point of convergence. This is new to our times. With it come new responsibilities to forge ahead.

Response to David Shannon

Sonya A. Quitslund

Dr. Shannon has presented us with an honest and yet encouraging view of the state of ecumenism as viewed from a Baptist perspective: honest because he does not try to gloss over the serious obstacles that still separate us, encouraging because he sees a genuine and profound shift in focus and commitment of energies from the pre–Vatican II emphasis to the post–Vatican II stress on *"recognition, acknowledgment,* and *celebration* of unity as one body in Christ."

An event such as we celebrate, the twenty-fifth anniversary of the promulgation of the Second Vatican Council's Decree on Ecumenism, can easily lend itself to a resurgence of triumphalism. Hence, if one were to find fault with Dr. Shannon's excellent and interesting presentation of the progress made in Roman Catholic-Baptist dialogue since 1984, it might be with his declaration that "Vatican II has greatly enhanced the meaning and significance of the ecumenical movement in our times." Perhaps he makes this statement primarily as a Baptist rather than as an ecumenist, for the Baptist-Catholic dialogue certainly

Sonya Quitslund is Professor of Theology at George Washington University in the District of Columbia.

is of recent vintage. Others, however, engaged in ecumenism over a longer time frame may not share his optimistic assessment. Have we really made that much more progress in the 1980s than in the '60s or '70s? How does one measure progress, let alone meaning and significance?

To look at Catholic ecumenism from a somewhat broader perspective and yet to build on the content of Dr. Shannon's paper, I would like to share some reflections from a historical perspective on his five "negative observations" concerning the decree that will perhaps shed additional light on the complexity of the whole ecumenical venture.

In addition to Leo XIII and Benedict XV, both keenly interested in unity and promoters of the Octave of Prayer for Christian Unity (the forerunner of the current Universal Week of Prayer for Christian Unity), it is fitting to recall the efforts of men like Lord Halifax, an Anglican, and Fernand Portal, a French Lazarist priest, true precursors to the modern movement, as well as the Benedictine Gerard Van Caloen who envisaged an outreach to the Greek Orthodox during Leo XIII's pontificate. With the condemnation of Anglican Orders, the embryonic movement came to a screeching halt in the 1890s, and both Catholic and Anglican ecumenists turned toward Eastern Orthodoxy, but with mixed results. Several decades later the possibility of semi-official Anglo-Roman Catholic talks under the sponsorship of the Cardinal of Malines-Brussels (Belgium), Desiree Mercier, sparked new enthusiasm in Halifax, but not in his Lazarist colleague. Halifax could not understand Portal's reticence. In the interim, Portal had become convinced that true ecumenism could proceed only if all Christian churches were directly involved. In short, he considered bilateral efforts doomed in advance.

This actually proved true of the Malines Conversations, because the highest authorities in both churches hesitated to become publicly identified with something that might ultimately fail, and fail it did. Rome could accept only one solution: return to or reunion with Rome. In the course of the Conversations, Mercier presented a paper that went counter to the prevailing Roman view. It became known as "United not Absorbed," and eventually contributed to the ecumenical downfall and ecclesiastical disgrace of its true author, Lambert Beauduin.

Shortly after drafting the paper, Beauduin met Angelo Roncalli, later Pope John XXIII. This chance encounter turned into a lasting friendship. Roncalli later acknowledged his ecumenical indebtedness to the monk. And the monk in turn, during Pius XII's reign, prophesied that Roncalli would be the next pope and that his first act would be to call an ecumenical council. Beauduin, years ahead of his church, recognized ecclesial reality in churches separated from Rome and argued for their recognition. Union, not reunion or return, alone made sense. When he arrived in Rome in 1921, Protestants and Orthodox were still listed as heretics and schismatics in his notes, but when he left in 1925 he considered them "brothers," even if "separated." He then founded a monastery whose explicit purpose was the "*Union* of Churches," a term rejected by many in Rome as patently heretical. The encyclical *Mortalium animos* of 1928, and later the *Monitum* of 1948, effectively put the damper on Catholic ecumenism. Nonetheless a new generation of ecumenists kept the ideas and ideals of pioneers like Portal and Beauduin alive.

Now, to return to Dr. Shannon's five negative observations:

1. Leo XIII introduced the use of the term "separated brethren" in official church documents in 1896. In *Satis cognitum* it was used to avoid wounding other Christians by calling them heretics or schismatics. This innovation did not catch on overnight. Hence, when the decree uses such terms it is affirming its continuity with Leo as well as with Portal and Beauduin. Some of the key framers of the language of the decree had been influenced in one way or another by Beauduin—as his students or as members of the very monastery he had founded. To a Protestant, "separated brethren" may sound triumphalist, but it represented a major advance in Rome when one recalls the 1890s and the 1948 Vatican suspicions concerning the then newly formed World Council of Churches. In 1964 it intended

to affirm a continuity with this earlier ecumenical history. Were it written today, we would substitute "fellow Christians" or "Christian brothers and sisters" for "separated brethren."

2. The pro-Western bias of the decree undoubtedly reveals where the framers came from as well as their earlier behind-the-scenes ecumenical efforts that focused almost exclusively on the Russian Orthodox after the Russian Revolution of 1917, and on the mass exodus of Orthodox into Western Europe. Of course, disciples of Halifax, Portal, and Beauduin tried to keep the movement alive and continued their interest not only in all Orthodox but in Protestants too. However, they had to be careful lest they jeopardize the future of the movement by seeming to reach out too far and too fast. In fact, while certain forces in Rome were busy building a case against Beauduin and his concept of union, this ecumenical prophet traveled extensively in Eastern Europe and the Near East, with extended stays in Palestine, Egypt, and Greece.

In Egypt in particular he was impressed with what an Anglican was doing to aid Coptic spirituality and theological growth. Of perhaps greater significance to us today is the interest he took in informing himself about Judaism and Islam. Both religions left a deep impression on him. He was to have made a full report on this trip to Rome, but upon his return he found himself on trial. Subsequently he was sent to do two years' penance for his ecumenical views, forbidden to write on ecumenical topics, and exiled from Belgium and his monastery for twenty years! One can only speculate on what new directions ecumenism might have had if the climate had been different in Rome. If the decree has some limitations regarding its recognition of smaller and older churches, it simply reflects the history that preceded it.

3. The decree does not address issues of praxis. Perhaps this reflects the view held by increasing numbers of those who have been involved in the movement for years, namely Christian unity ultimately will be the work of the Holy Spirit. Planning for the future is risky business; it rarely turns out as we expect. Attempts to devise suitable structures for the future united

church—for example, The Consultation on Church Union's original plan—just do not seem to work. Is it naive to suggest we follow the New Testament? It shows that different forms of polity emerged to suit different sets of circumstances, as needed. Unity in dogma and sacraments, in the final analysis, seems much more crucial than spending time arguing over incidentals that at best will probably affect a future generation and not the present. If we can agree to recognize each other fully as Christians, the rest will be elementary and perhaps end up an explicit endorsement of Beauduin's "United not Absorbed."

4. That the decree does not identify processes for interchurch interaction except through dialogue and mutual cooperation in social action should bring sighs of relief from all sides. Ecumenism should not represent some straitjacket solution into which we must fit ourselves. Ecumenism, like the constitutions of individual churches, is not an end in itself but only a means to carry out more effectively the mission Christ confided to his followers: Go, preach, and baptize. If the liberation theologians have taught us anything, it is that respect for human dignity means we let the people themselves decide what is best for them. We hope to be moving into a postpaternalistic world where people will be allowed to think for themselves. The ecumenical movement ought to be a leader in this.

As we work together in social action, we will learn to pray together without someone setting up structures to tell us how. Christ's words "Where two or three are gathered in my name, there I am" should be all the structure and encouragement that we need. Is it possible that those engaged in bilateral dialogue are hoping to accomplish more than Christ ever expected?

5. Finally, the decree places more emphasis on ecclesiology than upon issues of love, peace, and justice. Dr. Shannon is certainly justified in saying their integration into the decree would strengthen ecumenism's identity with such concerns. Is the decree perhaps a victim of its time reflecting the historical limitations of those times? We need to recall that the last two chapters of the first draft of the decree became the Declaration on the Relation of the Church to Non-Christian Religions and

the Declaration on Religious Freedom. The Declaration on Religious Freedom is grounded on the concept of human dignity, and the Declaration on Non-Christian Religions gives an even deeper basis for religious freedom in that it recognizes that truth can come from sources other than the Judaeo-Christian revelation. In short, to silence someone speaking specifically out of a religious tradition is in a sense to silence God. Can we afford to take that risk?

We need to recall the decree's focus on a pilgrim church moving toward Christ. In that context we need to continue admitting our guilt in preserving barriers to unity, whether as individuals or as churches. Certainly imprudence can harm the cause of unity, but so can excessive prudence. We should go forward without obstructing the ways of Divine Providence and without prejudging the future inspiration of the Holy Spirit. The decree expected that there would be a need to update our outreach as methods and approaches became out-of-date, or realized their full potential. Shortly before he died, Portal acknowledged he had done all he could and that new ideas from new sources were needed to move the movement forward: What was my work is finished. I no longer have anything to do but disappear. To go further, other means that I cannot imagine are needed (Ladous, *Monsieur Portal,* p. 475). Perhaps some of our religious leaders and ecumenists need to reflect on these words!

It may well be that Dr. Shannon, and the Baptist community he represents that has more recently entered into serious dialogue, will be the very ones to bring new ideas and methods to this most important enterprise. Those engaged in dialogue now struggle with trying to reconcile different ecclesiologies, with sensitizing their respective communities to the need "to exercise greater vigilance to ensure respect for religious liberty," and with scrutinizing carefully the implications of the development of doctrine for our traditions. They seek to work for a common understanding of that most fundamental of sacraments: baptism. But is this the only approach?

Last but not least, perhaps dialogue with a tradition that has a long, esteemed, and independent black tradition will help

American Roman Catholics better understand and appreciate the uniqueness of their fellow black Catholics. Until we Catholics fully understand the vast richness of our own ethnically varied Catholic Church in the USA and live in harmony with our own diversity, it is hard to understand how we can realistically hope to further the ecumenical movement. In the final analysis, it is not something we as Catholics or as Baptists accomplish, but something that we will do together as Christians in a true *leitourgia:* celebrate our oneness in diversity.

Twenty-five Years of Interchurch Relations: A Report

Thaddeus D. Horgan, S.A.

One of the primary objectives of the Second Vatican Council was to commit the Roman Catholic Church in our times to the quest for full visible unity among all Christians in the one church. In November 1964 the council's participants issued the Decree on Ecumenism, *Unitatis redintegratio,* which launched the Roman Catholic Church into the modern ecumenical movement. It set forth the principles by which Catholics would engage in ecumenical activities and projected the Catholic Church's vision of what Christian unity means. Since then the church has wholeheartedly committed itself to the ecumenical quest, particularly in its leadership at the international and national levels.

Here, in a summary way and from a Roman Catholic perspective, I wish to share just what those activities have been and are, especially those accomplished in the United States. I

Thaddeus D. Horgan, S.A., was until his death in April 1990 Associate Director of the National Conference of Catholic Bishops' Secretariat for Ecumenical and Interfaith Affairs and one of the five Roman Catholic members of the Faith and Order Commission of the National Council of Churches.

will suggest what they have taught us and what are some indications of future directions. Reviewing the past twenty-five years will, I hope, excite us to a new resolve to realize further the goal of Christian unity. As communications become more instant and as the global village becomes more a global neighborhood, the necessity of Christian unity "that the world may believe" becomes more imperative.

What We Have Learned

Ecumenical experience and activity have taught us much about what enkindles and sustains ecumenical life. The following lessons stand out as the more important:

1. A sense of holy discontent with disunity, perceived as a grace of the Holy Spirit, is the beginning of ecumenical commitment. This is sustained by deliberate daily prayer for Christian unity.

2. One has to enter the ecumenical arena without a specifically pre-arranged agenda and with a willingness to be surprised by where the Holy Spirit may lead. Therefore prayer is essential to ecumenical activity so that we stay attuned to the will of God for the church, the churches, and the entire human family.

3. Fidelity to one's own tradition is necessary for authentic ecumenical involvement. Only the person committed to his or her tradition can present it faithfully and uncompromisingly. This fidelity also enables one to appreciate what is authentic in one's partner(s)' tradition(s).

4. Ecumenism requires that we speak the truth with clarity and in charity, always aware that we seek Christian unity "so that the world may believe" (John 17:21-23). For the world to believe, efforts to achieve Christian unity even now must visibly witness to the gospel in the larger human community. Ecumenical activity should manifest God's reconciliation with humanity and God's will that all live in freedom, with dignity, and in justice.

5. Diversity will be characteristic of the united church. This is already evident in some of the concrete results of ecumenical activity. Attempts to merge churches from different traditions have not been very successful. Churches in the same tradition, however, have reunited. This was demonstrated in the USA in the past five years when two Presbyterian churches reunited and in the merger of three Lutheran churches into the Evangelical Lutheran Church. Churches working for specific unity with others of differing traditions, for example those in COCU, have formed covenant partnerships that preserve the specific gifts of each church rather than blend them together.

6. Theological education has become, and will continue to become, more ecumenical. So too has biblical scholarship, church history, and the study of liturgy. We hope this will produce a more ecumenically minded clergy as it becomes more widespread.

7. Leadership, especially at the local level, is essential to ecumenical progress. When an ecumenically sensitive bishop or pastor is replaced by one who is not, invariably ecumenical involvement comes to a halt—or if it continues, what the Decree on Ecumenism calls "false irenicism," that attitude that allows compromise for the sake of unity, invariably develops. In either case a gap often forms between the people and their designated leaders, making new starts all the more difficult.

Significant Developments

Spiritual Ecumenism

The Catholic Church has placed a priority on spiritual ecumenism, calling it the "soul" of the ecumenical movement. It is rooted in the Christian's commitment to genuine *metanoia,* a complete turning to God. In its ecumenical context it means reliance on the Holy Spirit as we do what we can for the reconciliation of separated Christians. It requires a profound prayer life and a stance before God that acknowledges our need for the grace of the Holy Spirit. It has had multiple practical expressions:

1. Christians do pray together, notably during the Week of Prayer for Christian Unity, on Martin Luther King Day, during Lent, on Palm Sunday, at civic occasions, and on Thanksgiving Day.

2. Christians engage in shared Bible study, not only at events like the National Workshop on Christian Unity but also in their local communities. Neighborhood shared prayer groups are not uncommon; nor is public prayer during a workshop service for a particular congregation of a different tradition. Mutual prayer is part of every local or regional "covenant relationship" that has been established between local congregations. A covenant relationship is an agreement between two or more parishes or congregations, or between dioceses and synods, from different church traditions, who pledge one another some degree of ongoing cooperation, support, and understanding. There are over a hundred of these in the United States at the present time.

3. Every session of the official interchurch theological dialogues includes times for joint prayer, as do the sessions of groups like the North American Academy of Ecumenists for theologians and educators, and the National Association of Ecumenical Staff for people involved in conferences of churches and similar organizations.

4. Clergy share in retreats and quiet days, and cooperate in preparing sermons or homilies in their local ministerial associations. *The Common Lectionary,* used by Roman Catholics, Episcopalians, Lutherans, Presbyterians, and United Methodists, among others, is usually enlisted as the basic text for this exercise. This makes it possible for the same passages of Scripture to be proclaimed and explained in our churches on the same day, despite our divisions.

5. The highest leaders of our churches have met formally in prayerful situations, often signing common declarations to promote the cause of unity between the churches. Pope John Paul II has included an ecumenical component in every one of

his pilgrimages, including the ecumenical prayer service at which he preached in Columbia, South Carolina, in 1987.

6. There has been a great outreach to other Christians by Roman Catholic retreat centers, monasteries, and other institutions that promote spiritual life. Other Christians have happily responded and use these facilities for their own religious enrichment.

Theological Ecumenism

Theological ecumenism is that scholarly research done by professional theologians whose explicit purpose is to overcome the apparent barriers to Christian unity. Ordinarily their reflection and research are done in bilateral or multilateral consultations organized by the churches. Eleven such dialogues are carried out in the USA. When theologians complete their task they issue an "agreed statement" on a topic, which is then referred to the leadership of the churches for evaluation and decision. At the present time the church is preparing responses to several of these agreed statements. Other churches have taken similar steps.

1. Theologians from most of the major Christian traditions (Lutheran, Reformed and Presbyterian, Pentecostal, Methodist, Eastern and Oriental Orthodox, Baptist, Roman Catholic, Disciples, Anglican, and the United Church of Christ) are engaged at some level in official dialogues. More than ninety Roman Catholics from the USA alone, men and women, laity and clergy, are involved. More and more multilateral discussions, such as the COCU (Church of Christ Uniting [formerly Consultation on Church Union]) or those carried out under the auspices of the Commissions on Faith and Order of both the World and National Councils of Churches, are taking place. Such bilateral dialogues, although they began long before the Catholic Church entered the ecumenical movement, are viewed today as the Roman Catholic Church's principal ecumenical activity. Its consistency in pursuing conversations on matters of faith and church order has been its major contribution to the modern ecumenical enterprise.

2. A remarkable number of agreements have already been achieved, indicating that we are on the pilgrimage toward that point where one day we will be able to start together to profess a common faith within one church. Where agreement has not been total, many feel that some progress toward convergence has nevertheless been made.

3. Churches that have not always been on friendly terms with one another are dialoguing in order to correct former misunderstandings or false views. Unfortunately, much more of this is needed in the USA.

4. Dialogues have begun to tackle ethical and moral issues because of the growing need for Christians to speak with one voice in the face of many technical developments that have moral implications. These dialogues, because they often deal with new issues about which some churches have not yet offered guidance to their members, often reveal that theologians agree or disagree not according to but across church traditions.

5. The "hierarchy of truth," which refers to the importance of doctrines based on their relationship to the central truth of faith, namely the life, death, resurrection, and ascension of Christ, has attained a certain prominence. Some theologians feel that total and complete unity on issues not at the core of faith does not constitute an obstacle to full communion. The possible practical implications of this are being discussed by church leadership and theologians.

6. *Koinonia* ecclesiology, or that appreciation of the church that sees it as a communion of persons gathered in the body of Christ—a visible praying, worshipping, and serving community of believers—has become the ecclesiology of the ecumenical movement. This is the ecclesiology that undergirds the documents of the Second Vatican Council. *Koinonia* is more and more the preferred image as the movement increasingly abandons the former language of total organic unity (merger or absorption). Theologians now speak of "corporate union" (a church retains its distinctiveness within a larger communion of mutually recognized "sister churches"), or of "conciliar fellowship"

(local churches retain their identity but are joined locally in a communion; each local communion belongs to a larger world-wide communion), or of "reconciled diversity" (sister churches act in communion with each other, but retain their divergent practices and even beliefs, provided these are not at the core of Christian faith).

7. Several ecumenical consortia of theological schools exist in many places around the USA. They allow for cross-registration by students, for the exchange of professors for some courses, and for deliberately planned gatherings for students and teachers alike to pray together, socialize, and enter into other joint projects.

Pastoral Ecumenism

This expression refers to ministries carried out in local dioceses and parishes/congregations by pastors and their associates. More and more these are areas of ecumenical involvement.

1. It is no longer surprising to have our church leaders, bishops, and judicatory heads issue joint pastoral letters on a variety of issues like prayer for unity, pornography, housing, and drug abuse. Frequently they join together in political advocacy for justice, especially at the state level.

2. Ministerial associations exist throughout the nation. One of their important functions is mutual pastoral support for priests and ministers themselves. Another is local planning for joint ecumenical programs involving people in their parishes/congregations.

3. Many nonsacramental pastoral ministries not only have been performed well by the laity but also have been performed ecumenically. Among these are ministries to shut-ins, visiting the sick, prison ministry, and care for the homeless and the hungry. This too is no longer considered exceptional or extraordinary.

4. Ecumenical offices and commissions have been established in most dioceses, synods, or church districts to develop

guidelines for ecumenical interaction and to assist local or regional leadership in their ecumenical activity. This has served considerably to advance local ecumenism.

Social Ecumenism

Common witness and service for God's people constitute social ecumenism. It is most often associated with the activities of conferences of churches, but not exclusively. Since the 1920s Christians have been urged to perform together their deeds of charity, relief work, and other social activities, unless their consciences forbade it. This is very appealing to many because it touches on the quality of their lives in their own towns or cities and even neighborhoods.

1. In 76 instances (out of 179) the various dioceses of the Roman Catholic Church across the USA are members of state, regional, city, and other local councils or conferences of churches. In some cases, as in Connecticut, Texas, and Illinois, all the dioceses of the state are members of the state conference of churches. These conferences, for the most part, are engaged in collaborative ministries and advocacy on behalf of the poor and powerless.

2. Many national organizations are ecumenical and inter-faith in their purpose and membership. These include Amnesty International, Bread for the World, and The Interchurch Center for Corporate Responsibility, among many others, that enable us in a variety of ways to be ecumenical.

Disappointing Developments

Spiritual Ecumenism

1. Religious prejudice, while greatly reduced, is still found in many places and in many churches. This indicates that the basis

of all ecumenical commitment, *metanoia* or a change of heart, is not yet as deeply rooted as one would wish. This, along with ecumenical insensitivity, has another side effect apart from hindering ecumenical life, and that is the "leakage" that occurs as people leave their churches. This frequently happens, for example, when couples that have entered religiously mixed marriages seek pastoral care for those marriages, especially when their children are born.

2. There is evidence that not only between churches but within them Christians do not accept one another's piety. This shows an ongoing lack of sensitivity to the religious and cultural influences on various styles of worship. In the USA we have traditional, African American, pentecostal, hispanic, Caribbean, "folk," and native American influences within most of our churches. It is questionable whether we have developed an openness to this diversity that goes much beyond lip service. Accommodating multiple styles of worship should be a sign of unity within diversity, not a divisive issue. Too often "taste" dictates what is judged "proper" or "right." This indicates that Christians—leaders, theologians, laity—have hardly begun to deal with cultural diversity itself, much less with its influence on the visible unity of the churches.

3. Prayer for unity has not been as widespread or as intense as the Decree on Ecumenism projects. Over the past ten years or so the Week of Prayer for Christian Unity appears to have lost some of its earlier zest. Correspondingly so has widespread concern for Christian unity.

4. The issue of intercommunion remains problematic especially at the local level. Roman Catholic canon law suggests a practice that safeguards the theological reasons why the Catholic Church does not have open communion, yet takes into account pastoral needs (cf. Canon 844.4). Total exclusion seems contrary to the spirit of that canon, yet that has been the interpretation and application of the canon in this country. In reaction to this absolutist viewpoint, some people wholly disregard the Catholic position on intercommunion.

Pastoral Ecumenism

1. Pastors often do not encourage joint pastoral (nonsacramental) ministries locally because they fear they could lose their people to another church. This is ironic because just this kind of ecumenical insensitivity is itself a cause of leakage. Ecumenically timid pastors are overlooking the power of collaborative witness in fulfilling the signs of the kingdom (Matt. 25:34ff.). And where this viewpoint prevails among the clergy one can be certain that there is no ecumenical formation of the laity either. The result is frustration for those who would be ecumenical and the loss of effective ministry.

2. The pastoral care of "ecumenical" (that is, religiously mixed) families has been getting some attention in recent times. But given the increasingly large number of interchurch marriages, much more is needed.

3. Unfortunately there are still some dioceses in the United States that lack ecumenical officers or functioning ecumenical commissions. Although they are in the minority, these are places in which Roman Catholic participation in ecumenical activity, if any, is at best symbolic. Obviously such a stance is contrary to the directives of the Catholic Church today.

Theological Ecumenism

1. We are currently at a turning point. The "easy" issues have been dealt with. Now the "hard" questions are on the agenda. Although some have said that theological ecumenism is locked in a stalemate, this is not necessarily so.

Many observers of the movement toward unity have a desire to see concrete results from the dialogues *now*. This puts pressure on church leadership. While we agree in theory that unity will be characterized by diversity, the issue now raised is: "What are the limits of diversity?" How diverse can our positions be without fracturing the very unity we seek to preserve?

The diversity I refer to here is not our differences on polity matters—the issue of a married clergy, for example—but our diversity on issues involved with the "hierarchy of truths." A more positive way to pose this challenge is to ask: "How much diversity/difference justifies our continuing the state of separation?" The answer to this challenge, along with our address to ethical and moral issues, is part of the unfinished theological agenda before the church and the churches.

Social Ecumenism

Three disappointments loom large in this category:

1. There is a continuing lack of participation by many local Roman Catholic dioceses in conferences of churches and other interchurch agencies.

2. Ethical issues should be the occasion for dialogue, but instead they sometimes become the cause of confrontation and greater divisiveness.

3. Too frequently we view the feminist movement and the agenda of the historic black churches as combative factors rather than as issues that might prod us beyond our present grasp of the concerns these churches and movements raise.

Key Frontiers for the Future

1. The most crucial area for the future development of ecumenical life is at the parish and congregational level. Ultimately it is here that Christian unity will or will not happen. As important as the decisions of church leaders may be, no matter how essential theological dialogue is, regardless of how involved we might be in actualizing the gospel message of liberation and human dignity across church lines, the most important place to experience unity with diversity is at the local level. This is why the already existing diversity within the Roman Catholic com-

munion should be emphasized and why Catholics should promote harmony between our multiethnic and multiracial parishioners. Emphasizing to the faithful the vast diversity within the one Catholic Church, as this is exemplified by the several Eastern Catholic churches, would also be very useful.

2. Local parish leadership should promote ecumenical neighborhood Bible study and shared prayer. This ought to be preceded by ecumenical education and training in the dynamics of sharing. How to be clearly and affirmatively Catholic, rather than apologetic or defensive or polemical, is the need. With this sort of ecumenical formation, the fear that Catholics will succumb to the proselytizing activities of others would prove groundless. Too often, the attempt to forbid Catholics from participating in ecumenical activities has only encouraged them to go anyway. This negative approach aids those who would try to draw Catholics from the church. It substantiates at the most local and practical level the tired accusation that Catholic clergy do not want the laity to read the Bible.

3. Nonsacramental ministries, particularly to nursing homes, hospitals, and prisons, as well as those performed on behalf of the homeless and hungry might be promoted more within ministerial associations so that local leadership will be manifestly united in supporting these ministries. In November 1989 the National Pastoral Life Center produced a cable teleconference over CTNA (the Catholic Television Network of America) to mark the twenty-fifth anniversary of the Decree on Ecumenism. It was evident from those who called in that at the local level ecumenism is alive and well, particularly in the area of joint ministry projects. They are so common that they are no longer newsworthy. Yet it seems much more can be done.

4. Local clergy could be examples of how local ecumenical discussions could take place among the laity. Unity in faith, not just in action, is the ecumenical goal. The laity need to be enabled and empowered to contribute to this aspect of the ecumenical enterprise. Local clergy who are theologically trained are in a position to lead others who are becoming more and more theologically acute. But a word of caution is in order.

These discussions, whether conducted among clergy or laity, are best not begun with the most burning issues before the churches. Too often, for example, "intercommunion" is the topic under discussion, but that is not a helpful place to begin.

5. At the level of official theological conversations by our churches we use two approaches. One is bilateral, in which two communions discuss particular issues with the hope of reconciling some of their differences. Only in a few instances have these dialogues led to a point of convergence. The other approach, the convergence approach, is associated with multilateral conversations. This was the method used by the World Council of Churches in the development of the landmark Lima Document (or BEM for Baptism, Eucharist, and Ministry Document). This may be a future direction for ecumenical conversations. Many analogous dialogues have considered the same issues, but isolated one from another. In Europe currently there are calls for the World Alliance of Reformed Churches, the Anglican Communion through the Archbishop of Canterbury's office, the World Methodist Council, and the Lutheran World Federation to effect multilateral conversations on issues that seem to have been resolved in bilateral dialogues. This may be the way for these churches to achieve full visible communion in fact.

6. There are three areas of faith and practice that recent multilateral conversations indicate are in greater need of clarification and common appreciation. These are the relationship between Scripture and the church (i.e., tradition), the meaning of sacrament and sacramentality in our various traditions, and the relationship of ministry (particularly ordained ministry) to the exercise of authority in our churches. In bilateral conversations papal primacy, infallibility, Mariology, the question of the ordination of women, and how authority functions are still in need of further study and resolution.

7. For all those involved in theological ecumenism the "hierarchy of truths" is a topic in need of further explication, particularly in view of its implied practical ecumenical results. Related to this is the issue of the "development of doctrine."

This is somewhat pressing because the dominant Western European-North American categories used in our discussions do not seen important to the local churches of the Catholic communion, and to the so-called Protestant younger churches, in the Third World. There is every indication that these will be the churches of influence in the next century.

8. Everyone active in the ecumenical movement must face the reality that both our nation and our world are "inter-religious." Christians should be one if we are to give an authentic witness to what our faith represents, and if we are to enter into conversations with adherents of other living faiths. The ecumenical horizon will embrace the issue of the unity of all humankind as well as the integrity of creation within the next decade. That process has in fact already begun.

9. Theological educators need to note this as well: today there are effective ecumenical consortia operating in the USA, but they offer little by way of practical or pastoral preparation for ecumenical or interfaith interaction, especially in Roman Catholic seminaries. As we enter a period when it seems there will be a greater emphasis on particular denominational identity, this becomes more significant. Denominational loyalty has come to mean very little to many Christians. This apparent indifference about specific religious affiliation has given rise to fundamentalism in Protestantism and conservative traditionalism in the Catholic and Orthodox churches as a way to reassert a specific denominational loyalty. Ecumenists also need to assert the importance of particular Christian identity and loyalty for ecumenical engagement. Yet we all must maintain a sense of openness to what is true and good in other religious traditions. Seminaries are a good place for developing these attitudes.

10. Finally the church needs to examine the issue of "reception," that is, the process by which the church integrates the results of the Second Vatican Council and of the ecumenical movement into the fabric of its living. Many Catholic and ecumenical developments of the past twenty-five years are influencing the life of the church and the churches. The reality of modern communications and how they are managed are

intrinsic to any consideration of how the people receive current church teaching, guidance, and experience. A mastery of these processes will be even more important in the years ahead. Just how the church and the churches develop in these years depends a great deal on how we handle the techniques and technologies of our own day.

Conclusion

Twenty-five years after the promulgation of the Decree on Ecumenism we find ourselves in a completely new situation, one deeply affected by the council and by the Roman Catholic Church's entrance into the ecumenical movement. Looking back we note the extraordinary advances that have occurred on all fronts. They sometimes overwhelm us. They certainly challenge us. They probably make us uncomfortable. But above all they leave us with a sense of "holy impatience" to press on to see where the Holy Spirit is leading the church, the churches, and this world we inhabit. From that perspective there are no limits to our hope.

Reflections on Twenty-five Years after the Decree on Ecumenism

James Crumley

A reassessment of the ecumenical scene in the twenty-five years since the Second Vatican Council and the Decree on Ecumenism is not simple. The impact of this document has been so extensive that one might conclude that the ecumenical movement began there. That would not be accurate, however, for the impetus toward the visible expression of the unity of the church extends back well before the last twenty-five years. There has, however, been remarkable ecumenical progress during this period. Clearly and openly, the Roman Catholic Church declared at the Second Vatican Council its vision and its commitment to work with others toward that goal that Jesus Christ himself expressed in the high priestly prayer. The action of the Roman Catholic Church not only added nerve to those who had already been attempting to relate to one another in common endeavor but also brought a new and powerful addition to the arena. The adoption of the Decree on Ecumenism has to be seen as the most important single event in the somewhat

---

James Crumley was the Presiding Bishop of the former Lutheran Church in America. He lives in active retirement in Leesville, South Carolina.

checkered history of the ecumenical movement. I believe it even
more important than the formation of some of the ecumenical
organizations that had been hard at work for several years.

One must not underestimate the impact when, in the
decree, the Roman Catholic Church addressed other groups of
Christians as "Churches and ecclesial communities" (19). Or,
further, when it declared that the one, holy, catholic, and
apostolic church "subsists in" (4) the Catholic Church but is not
limited to it. This way of addressing other Christians was not
only new but also more significant than we may realize today.
These words meant that the Catholic Church acknowledged a
kind of recognition of other churches and that it admitted the
Spirit to be active in them. Doors were then opened for actions
in many different directions.

More importantly, with the promulgation of the decree
the goal of unity became more clearly focused than had earlier
been the case in the ecumenical movement. True, many leaders
and some churches had expressed the goal of "full communion"
with one another, but not much progress had been made toward
it anywhere. Most had become satisfied with cooperation in
various projects, and the fundamental relationship between the
churches often assumed a much lower rank. The Second Vatican Council made quite clear not only that the movement was
a matter of action, cooperation, and goodwill but also that the
basic task was theological, involving the understanding of the
church and her nature. Not only did this position make an
important difference in the way in which this new partner
entered the ecumenical scene but also it undergirded those who
through the years had attempted to uphold the importance of
such an approach. It is not difficult to surmise that the important work of Faith and Order—Baptism, Eucharist, and Ministry—received encouragement and new possibilities from this
approach. After all, the Roman Catholic Church had been a
member of that organization, but now its members had a clear
direction, which other churches gladly adopted.

That Christians already have a relationship, a unity with
one another, is acknowledged in the decree. The church is

centered in its Lord Jesus Christ, and the Spirit has worked in many persons to bring them to faith in him. Baptism in the name of the triune God is recognized as effective as it has been practiced in many churches, and it is initiation into the church. Therefore, those who have been baptized have a relationship, God-given, with one another. That cannot be denied.

Further, there has to be a unity of prayer, for it is the one God to whom the baptized pray. Pope John Paul II has often spoken of the unity that we have in prayer and that it is through prayer that God will reveal the next steps that we ought to take toward and with one another. But, important as that fellowship is, it is not the total fulfillment of the goal of unity. That has to center in the Supper of our Lord, and until Christians can be together fully at the altar, there is still a longing for unity. One must agree wholeheartedly with the pope when he said: "Communion in prayer will lead us to full communion in the eucharist. I venture to hope that this day is near."[1]

It is important to note that the task of unity is theological, but there are also pastoral dimensions apart from the pursuit of theological agreement. That applies equally—and with a sense of urgency—to goal, method, and motivation. I have especially appreciated this emphasis made by John Paul II, one with which I have often expressed my full agreement.

For these very reasons the task of promoting unity must be seen as essentially a pastoral task. As long as Christians are divided, so long will the work of preaching the gospel be hampered; divisions among Christians impair the credibility of the gospel, the credibility of Christ himself. Disunity is a scandal, a hindrance to the spread of the gospel; it is our duty to strive by God's grace to overcome it as soon as we can.[2] This service of unity is a service of Christ, of the gospel, and of all humanity. It is, then, a truly pastoral service.[3]

1. John Paul II, *Addresses and Homilies on Ecumenism, 1978-1980,* ed. by J. Sheerin and J. Hotchkin (Washington, D.C.: U.S. Catholic Conference, 1981), 66.
2. Ibid., 55.
3. Ibid., 54.

The Decree on Ecumenism made possible new initiatives in the ecumenical movement. What progress has been made in those fields in these twenty-five years?

I look first at the theological dialogues. We Lutherans have felt from the beginning that the theological task is the primary one, and we have been delighted to find a dialogue partner who values a similar priority. Thus, the establishment of the Secretariat (now Pontifical Council) for Promoting Christian Unity in 1960 and the work of many bilateral and multilateral conversations are significant. Lutherans were especially glad to enter into that task early and with care and fervor. They understood from the beginning that the purpose of the conversation itself was to attempt to find areas of agreement and consensus. They were glad to examine again and reevaluate the significance of the issues that had caused and maintained the separation for these many years.

From the beginning dialogue helped to clarify the problems and assisted in getting rid of some stereotypes. From this side of the publication of the decree, it is not always easy to remember that the churches had not conversed with one another seriously for more than four centuries. Many sixteenth-century polemics had continued to color our attitudes toward one another. It is amazing, in truth, that the dialogues had such a good start and that they made progress from the beginning.

I am inclined nonetheless to wonder whether the right questions have been discussed in each instance. Of course, there were problems that have been church-dividing for several centuries that needed to be clarified and investigated to determine whether they were still relevant and seen in the same way as before. Perhaps that process has led to the consideration of the different priorities that ought to be placed on certain issues. Furthermore, would progress have been even more substantial if we had devoted more time to those doctrines on which we would have had agreement from the beginning? Are we really convinced that what we have in common is far broader and deeper than we sometimes admit? Where are the crucial issues of faith and life? The decree discusses this in article 11:

Furthermore, in ecumenical dialogue, Catholic theologians, standing fast by the teaching of the Church, yet searching together with separated brethren into the divine mysteries, should do so with love for the truth, with charity, and with humility. When comparing doctrines with one another, they should remember that in Catholic doctrine there exists an order or "hierarchy" of truths, since they vary in their relation to the foundation of the Christian faith.

In the spirit in which the dialogues have been held, each church's confessional position has become clearer to its own members. If one is determined first of all not to win a point, but to understand as clearly and deeply as possible the issues under consideration and from the many different points of view, it becomes possible to appreciate more fully one's own confession. It has been expected of dialogue participants that they will not work merely in an irenic manner intended not to offend each other, but that they will work in an open way that investigates fully the matters under consideration.

Let it be said as well that the theology and theological methods of the dialogues have been competently executed. I enjoy teaching the documents that resulted from the dialogues because they are obviously the creative and cutting edge of theological work today. The church bodies have named some of their most theologically skilled persons to this task. Their work has proceeded with both a sense of urgency and a deliberateness derived from a sense of the importance that attaches to this endeavor.

With deep satisfaction and with thanksgiving we point to two other important results—not just the process itself, but results. One is that there has been a developing consensus on many points. Few Lutherans would have thought just a few years ago that the doctrine of justification by faith might actually be said by some Roman Catholic and Lutheran theologians to be no longer *the* church-dividing issue. Involved in this agreement is a fundamental affirmation: our entire hope of justification and salvation rests on Christ Jesus and on the gospel whereby the good news of God's merciful action in Christ is made known; we do not place our ultimate trust in anything other than God's promise and saving work in Christ.

Also of great consequence is the reevaluation of the polemical attitudes and language of a former time and the removal, or possible removal, of the condemnations that were expressed in sixteenth-century documents. We are realizing anew that many of the doctrinal disagreements that have separated our churches in the past are beginning to disappear. Those controversies arose in a world very different from the present. Consequently it has become to a large extent impossible to make use of a past understanding of the world in the context of our present proclamation. Thus many of our traditional doctrinal disagreements are losing importance.

We should also note that on the local level there have been many instances of increasing fellowship and cooperative ventures. That has been fostered by the spirit and attitude expressed in the decree, and also by the way in which the churches have responded to the opportunities offered in this new climate. In the United States, the bishops of the Lutheran and Roman Catholic Churches developed a liturgy to be used for joint worship. The need for such a service was apparent as we witnessed more and more occasions for the faithful to worship together.

What are the most pressing issues remaining?

The first is a continuation of what is already taking place, especially the ongoing dialogues. Theological exploration and research must take place and should continue even if a total consensus were to be reached, something that none of us, I suspect, sees as realistic.

We are only beginning the process of reception and we do not fully understand just what is involved. But of necessity the church bodies that have appointed the dialogue teams and overseen their work need to pass judgment on the results. In the dialogue in the United States between Lutherans and Roman Catholics, a whole library of resources was developed over a period of more than twenty years. Only in the last few years of its life did the Lutheran Church in America begin to examine the results and take official action about them. Perhaps we were goaded into doing so by the request in Baptism, Eucharist, and Ministry that the document be acted upon by the churches at their highest level of authority. Otherwise, how can we know whether progress is being made or not? The churches themselves need to recognize a consensus when indeed it has developed, and need to give some guidance about the problems that remain after a period of work. The churches, not just the participants in a team, are in dialogue with one another, and their official actions ought to recognize that truth.

I am also firmly convinced that we must find levels of fellowship and action that are appropriate for joint cooperation. I am concerned that some insist that eucharistic fellowship cannot take place until there is total doctrinal agreement. After all, the eucharist is the sacrament of unity. True, but what do we mean by such agreement and who will determine when it has or has not taken place? I have often marveled that there is no full agreement among the faithful even in a particular church on this issue. Imagine polling one hundred worshippers as they came to the altar on their theological understanding of what is taking place. Would you expect to find unanimity among them? Or, even, would you venture that each of those disciples gathered around the table in the Upper Room knew exactly what Jesus was doing and what was intended by his action? Is it not true that controversies later arose among them as to what was taking place when that supper was again celebrated?

My point is simple. As firmly committed as I am to the theological enterprise, to the search for truth, and to clarity in expression, I have to recognize that theology and faith are sometimes not the same thing. Every priest or pastor has known persons of simple, trusting faith, but with no background in the academic discipline needed for theological articulation. But the point is they know the Lord Jesus Christ. And, in knowing that Christ, they reach out to one another.

Thus, I have to ask, are there not ways in which our being together in faith is not only a goal but also a part of the process

toward that goal? In the United States, the interim arrangement
for sharing the eucharist between Lutherans and Episcopalians
has been based on exactly that premise. The eucharist is a goal
of unity, but it is also a resource given by the Lord Jesus himself
for expressing the unity (cf. Decree on Ecumenism, 2; 8).

Further, the goal of "full communion" must always be kept
before us. Our consciousness of the demand for unity must not
wax nor wane, nor run in cycles, but it must be constant. There
are those who grow weary of the whole enterprise, some because
they think we have talked long enough and made enough
progress, others because they feel that the cause was impossible
from the beginning. It is important to name the fallacy in each
so that we will continue to express that which is deep within us
through the work of the Spirit.

The unity of the church demands renewal in the present
churches. The decree strongly emphasizes this point, and it
must be repeated. The command for unity is not the only
mandate under which we live out our discipleship, and the
record of each of us reflects both accomplishments and failure.
We do not wait for the full unity of the church to be expressed
before we with full intent and commitment live out our faith,
both personally and corporately.

The spirit of the Decree on Ecumenism as well as the task
it laid before us is well summarized in my opinion by Pope John
Paul II:

> All due thankfulness for what we have in common and what
> unites us cannot blind us to what yet divides us. We should in
> the best manner possible look not only to what may further
> divide us but rather to what transcends the division. We cannot
> simply stop with the affirmation, "We are and remain forever
> divided and in opposition to one another." We are called to tend
> to one another, in a dialogue of truth and of love, toward full
> unity in the faith. Only full unity gives us the possibility of
> coming together with the same mind and the same faith at the
> one table of our Lord.[4]

4. Ibid., 158-59.

The Decree on Ecumenism and
Its Ecclesiological Significance

Günther Gassmann

"The Decree on Ecumenism—Ten Years Later" is the title of
the report of an international ecumenical colloquium held in
Rome in 1974. The colloquium was organized by the Institute
for Ecumenical Research in Strasbourg, France, and by the
Pontifical International Institute of San Anselmo in Rome (the
report and documentation are published in Gerard Békés and
Vilmos Vajta, eds., *Unitatis Redintegratio 1964-1974* [Frankfurt:
Knecht und Lembeck; Rome: Studia Anselmiana, 1977]). The
report of the meeting, for whose final editing Harding Meyer
and I were responsible, focused on the remarkable ecumenical
developments, especially in the area of bilateral dialogues, in
the ten years following the promulgation of the decree. Today,
fifteen years later, one would have to repeat many of the
observations, questions, and hopes expressed in the report. Yet,
the greater distance in time leads me to assess the ecclesiological
significance of *Unitatis redintegratio* in a broader historical framework.

*Günther Gassmann is director of the Faith and Order Commission of the World
Council of Churches in Geneva, Switzerland.*

The Second Vatican Council was an eminent ecclesiological council, a council of the church on the church. This orientation was already implied in the intentions that moved Pope
John XXIII to his historic decision to summon it. All the conciliar documents are, in the specificity of their themes, ecclesiological explications and applications. Consequently, the impact of the council on the postconciliar period is predominantly
ecclesiological both in relation to the Roman Catholic Church
itself and to the ecumenical movement.

This emphasis was not accidental. In the decades before
Vatican II a lively and intense debate on ecclesiology dominated
the Roman Catholic theological scene. It was a spiritual ("the
Church awakes in souls," *Romano Guardini,* 1922) and theological struggle to liberate ecclesiology from its traditional confines
to merely serve as an apologetical, juridical-institutional self-
justification of the existing church. For the first time, fully
developed, biblically oriented, and theologically conceived ecclesiological concepts were presented. The principal expressions were the mystical body of Christ, the people of God, and
immediately preceding the council, the church as sacrament.
In this debate the church was brought back into history by
relating ecclesiology to the reality of the church (for example,
the rediscovery of the laity and the liturgical movement), to the
reality of the modern world (witness, mission, service) and,
finally, to God's saving and renewing history in the world. This
debate was influenced by non-Roman Catholic biblical and
theological scholarship and the emerging ecumenical movement. The encyclical *Mystici corporis* of 1943 took up elements
of the new ecclesiological movement and sought, at the same
time, to channel it with the traditional emphases of Roman
Catholic ecclesiology, especially in the identification of the Roman Catholic Church with the body of Christ.

One major aspect of the ecclesiological significance of
Vatican II was that it "received" these new developments in
ecclesiological thinking. The council legitimized them by "de-
creeing" (not defining in the strict dogmatic sense) for the first
time an ecclesiology for the Roman Catholic Church and

applied it in the different texts of the council to specific areas of self-understanding and life of this church. *Lumen gentium* articulated the fundamental assertions of this "reception" and *Unitatis redintegratio* has to be interpreted in the light—though not in the boundaries—of *Lumen gentium*. The specific ecclesiological significance of *Unitatis redintegratio*, however, lies in the fact that it further develops the new ecclesiological orientations in relation to the ecclesial reality outside the Roman Catholic Church, represented by the other churches and the ecumenical movement.

This radical change in perspective was prepared by *Lumen gentium*, which went beyond *Mystici corporis* by no longer claiming full identity between the church of Christ and the Roman Catholic Church. In a less exclusive manner, *Lumen gentium* (8) affirmed that the Church of Christ *subsists* in the Roman Catholic Church and acknowledged elements of true faith and grace among Christians separated from the Roman Catholic Church.

This still narrow gate was broadened by *Unitatis redintegratio*. The decree speaks not only of Christian individuals and elements of true faith but also of churches and ecclesial communities outside the Roman Catholic Church (19). The ecclesiological implications of the remarkable statement "that all who have been justified by faith in baptism are incorporated into Christ" are more far-reaching than the decree indicates (3). This common heritage is underlined and it is admitted that because of the divisions within Christianity the catholicity of the Roman Catholic Church is impaired (4). The need of reform and renewal of the church where one should also learn from others is emphasized (4; 5). While no definite description of the form of church unity is proposed, the relation between unity and diversity is affirmed (4). Most important is, of course, the "reception" of the ecumenical movement as "a movement fostered by the grace of the Holy Spirit" (1). All this is prefaced, as in *Lumen gentium*, by a trinitarian and especially christologically based understanding of the church of Jesus Christ and its unity (2), and in analogy to *Lumen gentium*, it is at the same time affirmed that "this unity, we believe, subsists in the Catholic Church" (4).

After decades of resisting the ecumenical movement before and after the encyclical *Mortalium animos* of 1928 many non-Roman Catholics have regarded this opening of the Roman Catholic Church toward other churches and the ecumenical movement as long overdue. They welcomed it as a positive development in twentieth-century history that was, however, still rather carefully limited in order not to obscure the self-understanding of the Roman Catholic Church as being the expression of the body of Christ. Yet that change and opening was much more revolutionary than these observers seemed to sense. The refusal to admit ecclesial reality outside the Roman Catholic Church and, consequently, the refusal to recognize in ecumenism a movement of churches struggling for the visible unity of Christ's church, had been an essential, even constitutive, element in traditional Roman Catholic ecclesiology up to *Mystici corporis* and Vatican II. The ecclesiologies of most other churches had not been conceived in this way, and the entry of these churches into the ecumenical movement required much less dramatic ecclesiological modifications. For the Roman Catholic Church, on the contrary, Vatican II and especially *Unitatis redintegratio* not only had opened a door to the outside Christian world but also had risked a far-reaching, and for many of its members disturbing, change in its own self-understanding. *Unitatis redintegratio* has become a historic document by announcing and initiating this historical and irreversible ecclesiological turning point.

The historical importance of certain decisions or documents in church history is rooted in their ability to receive, formulate, and legitimate new insights and developments. *Unitatis redintegratio* definitely belongs to this category of "landmarks." It does not diminish the significance of such landmarks that they are conditioned and shaped by a certain moment— even *kairos*—in history and are thus timebound in their language, concepts, and visions. This applies certainly also to *Unitatis redintegratio*. Yet this is only one side of the coin. Historical landmarks may be at the same time signposts pointing toward the future or opening up new ways into the future. And also in this sense *Unitatis redintegratio* is of permanent ecclesiological and ecumenical significance.

People are frequently—not without reason—skeptical about the effectiveness of long lists of recommendations in ecumenical and other documents. One must, however, admit that the second chapter of the decree, "The Practice of Ecumenism," has released—because many people were waiting for this—and encouraged an immense wave of new ecumenical activity since 1964. There were many efforts at reaching a better mutual understanding and respect as well as gatherings in common worship, witness, and social cooperation at many levels and on many occasions. I would like to underline especially the Roman Catholic initiatives in entering a growing number of bilateral dialogues at international and national levels and the official participation in the Faith and Order Commission of the WCC and thus in multilateral dialogue since 1968. Roman Catholic involvements are further evidenced in their increasing membership in national and regional councils of churches, and the full Roman Catholic sponsorship of the European Ecumenical Assembly on Peace with Justice in May 1989. All these forms of dialogue, membership, and cooperation imply a higher degree of ecclesial recognition than was expressed by *Unitatis redintegratio*. It is quite significant in this respect that the formulation that the baptized "are put in some, though imperfect, communion with the Catholic Church" (3) has been replaced by the much used formula of a real, though imperfect, communion between the churches in the ecumenical movement.

This progress beyond *Unitatis redintegratio* is confirmed by reflections on ecclesiology itself. Major elements of ecclesiology like the sacraments and the ministry of the church, and in recent years ecclesiology itself, have been the dominant topics of bilateral and multilateral dialogues in which the Roman Catholic Church has participated. This in itself represents a new stage. In *Lumen gentium* and *Unitatis redintegratio*, the ecclesiological reflection was a self-reflection with the aim of restating the identity of the Roman Catholic Church in a new constellation of church and world history. And this self-reflection provided also the basis and criteria for a fresh evaluation of the ecclesial and ecumenical reality outside the Roman Catholic Church. Now, in ecumenical dialogue on the church one can no longer speak of "outside" because the Roman Catholic Church has become participant in and part of a common dialogical reflection and search for an understanding of the nature and mission of the church. Such a dialogue presupposes a clear ecclesiological profile of the partners involved. But the dialogue will be a hopeless enterprise if such ecclesiological profiles become closed and static. The dynamics and purpose of the dialogue are to move toward common basic perspectives of ecclesiology that will enable the churches to move closer to each other.

The ecumenical dialogue on the church is very much enriched by the insights of Vatican II and ecclesiological developments since then. The concept of the church as sign and instrument or sacrament of God's purpose of salvation and reconciliation of all of humanity has entered ecumenical thinking. In recent years the understanding of the church as *koinonia* has been welcomed in bilateral dialogues and in the work of Faith and Order as a comprehensive ecclesiological orientation.

This concept is able to integrate theologically in a coherent way different aspects of ecclesiology such as the diverse biblical images of the church, the divine origin and nature of the church and its historical, institutional manifestation, the local and universal dimensions of the church, and the conciliar communion of churches as an expression of visible unity. This Roman Catholic contribution is complemented by the Protestant insistence on taking the church seriously as a historical and therefore ambivalent reality, and by the Orthodox emphasis on a eucharistic, pneumatological, and collegial ecclesiology.

Ecclesiology will remain a major preoccupation of ecumenical dialogue for some time. It has become obvious that several of the remaining main controversial issues like Scripture and tradition, teaching authority in the church, apostolic continuity, episcopal succession, and the role of the church in God's saving action can be most effectively addressed within the framework of ecclesiological convergence. But also the ecumenical process on "Justice, Peace, and the Integrity of Creation" requires such an ecclesiological convergence for the sake of common witness and service.

Given these developments, which clearly move beyond the positions and expectations of *Unitatis redintegratio,* I see in the expression that the church of Christ and its unity "subsists" in the Roman Catholic Church no barrier to further progress. On the contrary. This term and concept could perhaps provide for all churches the most adequate formula for expressing in a consistent way their relationship as historical entities to the body of Christ. Vatican II and especially *Unitatis redintegratio* have demonstrated that the tension between the confession of the one church of Jesus Christ and a plurality of churches can no longer be resolved by the claim of one or several of these churches to be the one and only manifestation of this one church. Furthermore, the terminology of other churches who speak of being a part of or of belonging to the body of Christ seems to me theologically inadequate or even misleading. Accordingly, the understanding that the mystical body of Christ transcends all our individual ecclesial communities and, at the same time, subsists in them provides a way forward. Full communion between the churches, which is the aim of ecumenical dialogue (and which does not necessarily imply the disappearance of ecclesial traditions by merging them) would then include the mutual recognition that the one mysterious body of Christ subsists in the different churches who through their communion together manifest this body.

Unitatis redintegratio has opened up new ecclesiological developments that have now taken on their own dynamic and ecumenical logic. Decisions of the church that enable such ways into the future will certainly remain historical landmarks.

Before and After the
Decree on Ecumenism of Vatican II

Michael A. Fahey, S.J.

When the Second Vatican Council opened in 1962 I was twenty-nine years old and had just completed my first year of theological studies. The next four years, especially in the fall months when the council was in session, were among the most exciting in my life. I still remember how after attending the morning mass I went directly to the commons room so as to be the first to read the single copy of the daily *New York Times* available to 150 Jesuits in which I could read about yesterday's doings at the council. The *New York Times*'s Vatican reporter in those years was the Jewish journalist, Irving R. Levine; his coverage of the council was excellent, especially when one recalls that all speeches were delivered in Latin and that the Vatican has a decidedly laid-back attitude toward the media. When reading those daily accounts of the debates on church, revelation, liturgy, and ecumenism, I felt a sense of drama otherwise lacking in my very isolated existence in those days.

Michael A. Fahey, S.J., is Dean of the Faculty of Theology, University of St. Michael's College, Toronto, Canada.

I read all the accounts of the council I could from sources ranging from the *National Catholic Reporter* to the *New Yorker* to the weekly English edition of the *Osservatore Romano.* Seminary life was opening up. Even our usually staid refectory reading was enlivened by Hans Küng's *The Council, Reform and Reunion,* a work that sparked our imagination. Other unlikely table reading included an essay entitled "A Time to Mend," a personal account by the retired dean of Harvard Divinity School, Douglas Horton, who was attending Vatican II as an observer for the International Congregational Council. As we ate our meals in silence, we listened attentively to installments of "Letters from Vatican City," the work of a mysterious author who went by the nom de plume Xavier Rynne.

Our readings as Catholic theology students in those days were carefully monitored. A book by a Protestant on biblical or theological topics required special permission of the Father Superior. When I had been appointed managing editor of *New Testament Abstracts,* I was in the anomalous position of receiving across my desk regularly 200 journals with a large number of articles, authored by non-Catholics, that I was not supposed to read. The Superior suggested that I write to the Father Provincial for general permission to read works by other Christians. This request was granted "on the proviso," so went his written reply, "that you remain in close contact with your spiritual father."

About this time I entertained my first fantasy about doing doctoral studies in ecumenism. I was attracted not to the usual place, Rome, but to the German universities where two faculties of theology, one Catholic, one Protestant, existed side by side. After poring over many a *Vorlesungsverzeichnis,* I decided to pursue my graduate studies at the University of Tübingen. By the time that Vatican II celebrated its closing ceremony I was enrolled at that Swabian university and preparing for courses taught not only by Küng, Ratzinger, and Schelkle but also by Käsemann, Moltmann, and Ebeling.

Even at our rustic American seminary, the council seemed to spur us to open doors to many more visiting lecturers from

the outside, including a previously unheard of number of Protestants. It was exciting to have Hans Küng in person in our
auditorium (especially since he had been banned in some cities),
as well as Karl Rahner, who spoke eloquently and without notes
in flawless Latin on Christian freedom and the New Testament
concept of bold speech. Between sessions in Rome, Catholic
hierarchs from Europe were traveling to North America to speak
of their experiences. For us these included Franz Cardinal König
of Vienna, who spoke not only of religious freedom but also of
his secret cloak-and-dagger meetings with Josef Cardinal Minds-
zenty in the Budapest US embassy where he was helping to
arrange his move to freedom. The year of my ordination, 1964,
we had a visit from one of the major drafters of the council's
Decree on Ecumenism, Augustin Cardinal Bea, S.J.

But the most exciting moments for us junior, aspiring
ecumenists were the visits of other Christians from Europe
(Joachim Jeremias, Max Lachmann, Oscar Cullmann, Hans
Conzelmann, and others). We also had a contingent of local
Protestants who spoke about changes in the Catholic Church:
William Wolf, George Huntston Williams, Krister Stendahl,
G. Ernest Wright, Albert C. Outler. I began to reason as follows:
Protestants are coming to our school and are even sitting in as
invited observers at the council, so why couldn't I spend a
summer at one of their divinity schools? I broached the request
about the possibility of attending a session at Union Theological
Seminary in New York City. I argued that these were "only"
Scripture and not dogma courses. To my delight the permission
was granted with the understanding that I not disguise my true
identity and would agree to wear my clerical "Roman collar," no
matter how hot Manhattan got. My summer courses at Union
with Professors Bernhard Anderson and J. W. Bowman were
biblical, but I stumbled upon Union's ecumenical library and its
growing special collection of agreed statements. My summer
passed with glorious hours there and with Union's periodical
collection where I read about what German Lutherans and Swiss
Reformed and British Anglicans and Belgian Catholics were
saying about the drafts and projects of Vatican II.

Our years in isolated study of theology were troubled by the death of Pope John XXIII (June 3, 1963, the day after Pentecost) after the first session. Would the council continue? And if so, under whom? The Cuban crisis had come and gone. But the assassination of John F. Kennedy troubled our November days with sadness and a sense of the tragic. We spent days of disbelief before the TV screen watching the funeral, including a Catholic funeral mass that seemed in its old form quite archaic.

During this period we were hearing much about a proposed decree on ecumenism. From November 26 to 29, 1962, during the first session of the council, a draft text theoretically on "ecumenism" was being discussed, but it was only a text about how Catholics should deal with the Eastern Orthodox Church. It was entitled *De unitate ecclesiae* and had been drawn up by the Commission for the Eastern Churches. By December 1, 1962 it was decided that this text would be combined with another schema, *De oecumenismo,* a draft being prepared by the newly established Secretariat for Promoting Christian Unity. This draft had five chapters (two of which provoked stormy discussion and which were moved into other decrees): (1) Principles of Catholic Ecumenism; (2) The Implementation of Ecumenism; (3) Christians Separated from the Catholic Church; (4) Attitudes of Catholics toward Non-Christians (particularly toward the Jews); and (5) Religious Freedom.

Between the first and the second session of the council in the first eight months of 1963 this text on ecumenism was circulated to the bishops at home. When this draft was discussed at the second session from November 18 to December 2, 1963, I remember the excitement and high drama reported in the press. These were critical days as they discussed the first three chapters of the draft. There was chagrin and discouragement by the majority in having to listen to opponents of ecumenism, cautious clerics who wanted great care exercised so as not to scandalize the simple faithful. One of the most forthright speeches was delivered in the council hall on November 26, 1963, by Bishop Stephen A. Leven, auxiliary bishop of San

Antonio, Texas, who spoke out strongly against the critics of ecumenism: "Again and again in this hall they continue to chastise us as if the prelates who feel compelled by clear evidence to acknowledge the gifts of the Holy Spirit in persons of other ecclesial bodies were denying the Faith and giving grave scandal to the innocent" (text in Floyd Anderson, ed., *Council Daybook: Vatican II, Sessions 1 and 2* [Washington: NCWC, 1965], 307).

It was concluded during this period that there could be no decree on ecumenism if the last two chapters on relations with the Jews and on religious freedom were included. There was certain to be a stormy discussion, so a decision was taken to refer these questions to separate decrees. The objections, the delays, the uneasiness felt by some led to a certain discouragement in the mood of the council.

Soon after this session I obtained permission to drive into downtown Boston to attend an evening public lecture at the Paulist Center on Park Street, where the pioneer American Catholic ecumenist, Gustave Weigel, S.J., was speaking on what he saw as the council's loss of nerve and vacillation. I was shaken by his discouragement and note of despondency. But I was shocked to read several weeks later that Weigel had died suddenly in New York City of a heart attack certainly brought on by the stress and overwork of his involvement with the council. Weigel also told us that many of the US bishops were shocked at some of the anti-ecumenical attitudes of some bishops who clearly had little firsthand experience of working with other Christians.

The third session of the council saw the final vote on the Decree on Ecumenism. A straw vote was taken on November 20, 1964, in which the tally was 2,054 in favor, 64 against, 11 invalid. The following day came the formal definitive vote, which tallied 2,156 in favor, 11 against. At the very last minute before the vote, Pope Paul VI introduced nineteen changes that he felt could be made without marring the text, but that would reassure certain vacillating bishops and thus make the vote almost unanimous. Some of the emendations made the professional ecumenists uneasy, but this was largely a difference in practical strategy. The text now became history and was no longer called *De oecumenismo* but rather by its formal name, *Unitatis redintegratio*. The full text of the document appeared in the *New York Times*. And we breathed a sigh of relief.

I mention some of these personal recollections because they help us (including myself) gain some perspective. I happen to be one of those who feel that ecumenism has lost some of its momentum, and I am glad to have Thomas Ryan's *Survival Guide for Ecumenically Minded Christians*. But when I concentrate not on whether we have assimilated all the nuances of the basically open text, but on the dramatic shift in the ecumenical environment, I see that the work of ecumenism has not failed but has become so commonplace that we lose perspective. The Catholic closed society that I considered part of the avant-garde of church life has for the majority of Catholics disappeared. Consider the creation of and continuance of our ecumenically based divinity schools, our broader reading, our bonds of friendship and collaboration with other Christians. This is so much a part of life among Catholics that it hardly goes noticed. Even the intemperate outbursts of the Traditionalists of Archbishop Lefebvre and the closing of ranks of neoconservatives are all the more noticeable because they stand out as going against the tide. The visits of Pope John Paul II to the World Council of Churches, to other Christians of India, his speeches to the Lutherans in Germany and the Nordic countries, especially Scandinavia, his close exchanges in the Vatican with the Ecumenical Patriarch and representatives of the Ancient Oriental Churches all show a dramatic paradigm shift.

Perhaps our own impatience with failure to get on with eucharistic hospitality, with mutual recognition of orders, with greater commitment to shared decision-making in matters doctrinal is a function of our recognition of how far we have come. My own conviction is that the slowdown at the international level will gradually encourage national hierarchies, the various "local churches," to move ahead even if on a worldwide basis there is failure to come to total agreement. The challenge of the ordination of women as priests and bishops will surely remain the most divisive issue, but it could in fact be a grace to help us reappropriate our deepest Christian tradition and to stir up within ourselves whatever in the Christian experience may have been forgotten.

All things considered, these twenty-five years have been a time for which to offer heartfelt thanks to God as we rededicate ourselves to the unfinished agenda.

The Theology of Communion as an Ecumenical Resource

Susan Wood, S.C.L.

The twenty-five years since the Second Vatican Council have witnessed a growing consensus that an ecclesiology of communion is the central and fundamental idea of the council's documents.[1] The category of "communion" is important in ecumenical discussion for two reasons: first, because it defines the church in terms of those elements of faith and grace that create community rather than ecclesiastical structures; second, because it also allows for degrees of unity among the various churches. Communion is, therefore, a much more elastic concept than church membership. In response to this consensus, this reflection on the Decree on Ecumenism examines the use of *communio* in the decree, notes the development of this concept of the church in recent ecumenical convergence statements on baptism and eucharist, and then comments on its implications for "full ecclesiastical communion."

1. "Final Report of the 1985 Synod of Bishops," *Origins* 15 (Dec. 19, 1985), 448.

Susan Wood, S.C.L., is Associate Professor of Theology at Saint Mary College, Leavenworth, Kansas.

Communio in the Decree on Ecumenism

The frequency with which the word "communion" occurs in the Decree on Ecumenism is striking. Indeed, "communion" is the measuring rod by which church unity is ascertained: restored unity is described as "full ecclesiastical communion" and partial unity as "imperfect communion."

One problem for the council was how to identify the Christian communities not in full union with the Roman Apostolic See. The solution was to refer to the separated communities in the East as "churches" and to those in the West as "separated churches and ecclesial communities" without attempting to define the difference. These communities were ecclesial insofar as they contained elements capable of creating and sustaining *communio,* such as the Scriptures as the Word of God; liturgical actions; faith, hope, and charity; the gifts of the Spirit; grace; and, preeminently, incorporation into Christ by baptism. Due to the presence of these elements, the decree acknowledges the corporate life of other Christian communities as being salvific and as having some kind of ecclesial reality. Significantly, despite the hesitation for various reasons to identify ecclesial communities in the West unambiguously as "churches," the decree does not hesitate to refer to them as "communions" (1; 4).

Many observers of the council questioned what form "full ecclesiastical communion" would assume. Early commentators, noting that the third chapter of the Decree on Ecumenism seems to describe other Christian churches and ecclesial communities "in terms of their degree of coincidence with the Roman Catholic Church," pointed to the decree's tension between a "Christologically centered and a Rome-centered ecumenism."[2] One fear of Protestant observers was that full ecclesiastical communion would be equated with a "return to Rome." The resolution of this tension between a christologically centered and a Rome-

---

2. José Míguez-Bonino in *The Ecumenical Review* (April 1965), 111, cited in Robert McAfee Brown, *The Ecumenical Revolution* (New York: Doubleday, 1967), 202.

centered ecumenism depends in part on whether this communion is envisioned as a communion between churches as institutions or as a communion that transcends, even though it does not bypass, the churches as institutions.

Two Models of Communion

Two separate but inadequately distinct models of communion are present in the decree: the dynamic interrelationship (*koinonia*) of Father, Son, and Spirit within the Trinity, and incorporation in Christ through baptism and eucharist. In the words of the decree, "It is the Holy Spirit, dwelling in those who believe and pervading and ruling over the entire Church, who brings about that wonderful communion of the faithful" (2). This model of church unity is expressed in Jesus' prayer "that all may be one; even as Thou, Father, art in me, and I in thee, that they also may be in us . . ." (John 17:21). This relationship of *koinonia* emphasizes the indwelling of the Trinity within the individual and that person's relationship with God.

This interior relationship of shared participation is objectified and made visible in the sacramental relationships, particularly in baptism and eucharist. It is by justification by faith in baptism that people are incorporated into Christ, have the right to be called Christians, and are accepted as brothers and sisters by those in the Catholic Church (3). The eucharist is the sacrament by which "the unity of the Church is both signified and brought about" (2). One of the breakthroughs in the decree is the recognition that even though the Roman Catholic Church does not recognize the validity of the eucharist in those ecclesial communities lacking proper apostolic succession, it does acknowledge that they commemorate the Lord's death and resurrection in the Holy Supper, and that this signifies life in communion with Christ (22). In other words, the decree acknowledges the salvific character of those celebrations of the Lord's Supper that it does not recognize as valid, an acknowledgment with rich implications for ecumenical dialogue on the eucharist.

These two models of unity, the *koinonia* of Father, Son, and Spirit, and the sacramental incorporation in Christ in baptism and the eucharist are not mutually exclusive, but they are not absolutely identical either. Contemporary sacramental theology does not view sacramental action as exclusively christological, isolated from the work of the Father and the Spirit. Yet the signification of the sacramental model possesses a tangibility, a visibility, not present in the other model. Furthermore, the sacramental model more clearly expresses the ecclesial implications of the relationship of *koinonia*. With baptism in Christ, one also becomes a member of the church, and the eucharist is constitutive of the church. The distinction and interrelationships between a communion based on the trinitarian interrelationship and one based on sacramental incorporation carry considerable significance for ecumenism, particularly when a strongly sacramental church is in dialogue with one which is less so.

Baptism and Eucharist in an Ecclesiology of Communion

Ecumenical documents on baptism and the eucharist since the Decree on Ecumenism have developed the ecclesial significance of these sacraments for the *communio* of the church. The Anglican-Orthodox USA Agreed Statement on the Eucharist (January 1988) notes that "the Eucharist is coming to be understood not only as a means of grace . . . but as expressive of the very nature of the Church . . . [and] makes it what it is called to be, manifesting and constituting the Church as the body of Christ, fashioned by the Spirit and called to participation in the very life of God."[3]

3. "Anglican-Orthodox, USA Agreed Statement on the Eucharist," *Ecumenical Trends* 17 (June 1988), 81. See also "The Ecclesial Nature of the Eucharist," A Report by the Joint Study Group of Representatives of the Roman Catholic Church in Scotland and the Scottish Episcopal Church, in *Called to Full Unity, Documents on Anglican-Roman Catholic Relations, 1966-1983*, Joseph W.

The consultation cites the Moscow Statement (par. 24): "The Eucharist actualizes the Church. The Church celebrating the Eucharist becomes fully itself; that is, koinonia, fellowship—communion." The World Council of Churches' Lima Document on Baptism, Eucharist, Ministry (BEM; Jan. 1982) does not express the ecclesial nature of the eucharist as strongly, although it states that "eucharistic communion with Christ who nourishes the life of the Church is at the same time communion within the body of Christ which is the Church" (I,D,19).

BEM expresses the communion effected by baptism with the observation that in baptism Christians are incorporated into Christ, the crucified and risen Lord, and that through baptism, Christians are "brought into union with Christ, with each other and with the Church of every time and place" (I,D,6). The Vatican criticizes this document for not giving reasons why baptism is an unrepeatable act, or why baptism is necessary for salvation.[4] An answer to these criticisms lies, in part, in a theology of an ecclesiology of communion.

When administered with water in the name of the Trinity, baptism is unrepeatable. This is rooted not only in the faithfulness of God, but also because it effects an incorporation in Christ and his church which is one and undivided despite a divided Christianity. The church of Christ into which the baptized are incorporated transcends its historical divisions. This is implicitly recognized in the Roman Catholic practice and the BEM recommendation of not rebaptizing a Christian already baptized in another denomination.

Baptism in the name of the Father, Son, and Spirit is ultimately necessary for salvation because it creates *communio,* and grace, considered as relational rather than some reified substance, is none other than this communion in the very life of the Trinity. This is never an individual communion, but an

---

Witmer and J. Robert Wright, eds. (Washington, D.C.: U.S. Catholic Conference, 1986), 73-94.

4. "Baptism, Eucharist and Ministry: An Appraisal," *Origins* 17 (Nov. 19, 1987), 402-6.

ecclesial communion, indicated by the fact that baptism confers membership in the church. According to traditional sacramental theology, sacraments effect grace by signifying, and what is signified is participation in the death and resurrection of Christ, a participation in his life which we call grace. This is why even "imperfect communion" is sanctifying, and the Decree on Ecumenism can say that liturgical actions of brethren divided from us can truly engender "a life of grace [and] can aptly give access to the communion of salvation" (3).[5] Thus intimate union with one another and the triune God in Christ constitutes final salvation. In patristic terms this ultimate union forms the "whole Christ," which is the Pauline body of Christ.

An ecclesiology of communion illumines the close relationship between baptism and eucharist, for both are the incorporation in Christ that is constitutive of the ecclesial community. Thus both are sacraments of initiation, and baptism finds its full culmination in the eucharist. The divisions in Christianity are experienced more acutely with regard to the eucharist than with baptism, indicating that the imperfect communion achieved results from a common baptism, while that communion still lacking obscures the unity signified by the eucharist.

Communion of Salvation

The significance of ecclesial communion for a theology of grace remains largely unexplored, but can help answer the question of how sacraments effect grace by extending the signification of a sacrament to its ecclesial dimension. Such a theology of grace illumines the connections between baptism, eucharist, church, and forgiveness of sins. Baptism and eucharist signify not only cleansing from sin and the body and blood of Christ offered as

5. These brief comments do not intend to exhaust the Roman Catholic theology of sacramental character, but intend merely to sketch the broad outlines of some of the applications of an ecclesiology of communion.

nourishment, but also the assumption of the identity "Christian" by participation (immersion) in the death and resurrection of Christ and incorporation into the body of Christ formed of those who partake of the one loaf (1 Cor. 10:17). Consequently, communion in Christ and the church becomes both a symbol and a reality of grace, while estrangement signifies and constitutes a condition of sin. Forgiveness of sin, much more than a juridical pronouncement of absolution, is essentially synonymous with the reconciliation of that union, simultaneously christological and ecclesial, that has been broken.

Communion of Communions

From what has been said, it should be clear that the primary emphasis of *communio* is neither organizational structure nor the fellowship of goodwill among Christians, but the elements of grace and sacrament that ultimately identify ecclesial communities in terms of their relationship to Christ. The council affirmed in the Dogmatic Constitution on the Church (*Lumen gentium*) that the church of Christ is present in local churches, for "in them the faithful are gathered together through the preaching of the gospel of Christ, and the mystery of the Lord's Supper is celebrated 'so that, by means of the flesh and blood of the Lord the whole brotherhood of the Body may be welded together'" (LG 26). Consequently, to consider the church as *communio* is to begin at the most local level. The dogmatic constitution identified this as the particular church since this was the "altar community" around its bishop, the parish church historically being an extension of this. The universal church is not the sum total of these particular churches because the church of Christ "subsists in" each particular church (LG 8). Structurally, then, the church is a communion of particular churches, each in union with each other and the bishop of Rome. This communion, fundamentally eucharistic, is objectified—one might also say sacramentalized—in the college of bishops. A bishop is constituted a member of the episcopal body "in virtue of the sacramental consecration and by the hierarchical communion with the head and members of the college" (LG 22). Further study needs to be done to clarify why and how the communion of particular churches, that interconnection between eucharistic communities, is sacramentalized through ministry when the eucharist is itself a sacrament of unity.

Within a theology of church as *communio,* one possible model for ecumenical unity would be to retain the identity of separated ecclesial communities as "communions." Since particular churches are identified by their eucharistic center, objectified in the person and office of the bishop, these "communions" would be recognized as "particular churches" based on common and mutual recognition of faith, sacramental practice, and ministry. The "communion of communions" model of church unity respects the diversity and individual identity of the participating ecclesial communities. Ecumenically, "full ecclesiastical communion" will be achieved, not when ecclesial communities separated from the Roman Apostolic See are absorbed into a monolithic Roman church, but when unity among all the particular churches is achieved.

The greatest obstacle to the realization of this model at this time lies in the diverse theologies and practice of church ministry and the related concepts of apostolic succession and Petrine ministry. Ministry is of significance not only for church governance and structure but also for mutual recognition of the eucharist. The theology of the particular church in Roman Catholicism rests heavily upon the episcopacy wherein the bishop functions as the representative of the local church and focus of ecclesial unity. Not all Christian ecclesial communities have retained the episcopacy. The advances toward convergence in faith and practice in baptism and eucharist, particularly with respect to their relation to ecclesial *communio,* in addition to the BEM recognition of the threefold ministry of bishop, presbyter, and deacon, mark important progress toward the realization of a "communion of communions." An ecclesiology of communion also indicates the areas in which further study, dialogue, and convergence are needed.

An Ecumenical Metaphor:
Mary and Elizabeth

J. Francis Stafford

Both Catholics and Protestants revere Westminster Abbey in London. Dating back to the dawn of the Catholic faith in England, the abbey for generations resounded with the Gregorian chant of Benedictine monks. All the English kings and queens since William I have been crowned there. Among the eighteen monarchs buried there, I wish to point out the tomb containing the remains of two sisters: Mary I, the Catholic queen, and Elizabeth I, the Protestant queen. The Latin inscription on the tomb is of special ecumenical interest: *Regno consortes et urna, hic obdormimus Elizabetta et Maria sorores in spe resurrectionis.* ("Sharing the same throne and tomb, here we sleep, Elizabeth and Mary, in the hope of the resurrection.") *In spe resurrectionis,* "in the hope of the resurrection," the two sisters sleep. This grave of the Catholic and Protestant queens, sisters together in the hope of the resurrection, can serve as a meta-

---

The Most Rev. J. Francis Stafford is the Archbishop of Denver, a member of the Vatican Congregation for the Doctrine of the Faith, Chairperson of the National Conference of Catholic Bishops' Committee for Ecumenical and Interfaith Affairs, and co-chair of the Lutheran-Roman Catholic Dialogue in the USA.

phor of the present state of Protestant and Catholic Christianity—both waiting the power of the Spirit of holiness who raised
Jesus from the dead to restore their ecclesial unity (Rom. 1:4).
I will return to this image later after noting the special significance of the anniversary we are celebrating.

November 21, 1964, marks a watershed in the life of the
Catholic Church. On that day, Pope Paul VI, together with the
2,148 fathers of the Second Vatican Council, affixed their sig-
natures to the conciliar decree *Unitatis redintegratio*. With this
the council, having already declared its teaching on the nature
of the church in the dogmatic constitution on the church, *Lumen
gentium,* and "moved by a desire for the restoration of unity
among all the followers of Christ . . . set before all Catholics
certain guidelines, helps, and methods, by which they too can
respond to the grace of this divine call" (1). With the words "by
which [Catholics] too can respond to the grace of this divine
call" to seek after the restoration of unity among all churches
and between all Christians, the council acknowledged that
others were already responding to God's initiative.

Some viewed the Catholic Church as a late arrival to the
ecumenical movement. However, since November 21, 1964, the
Catholic Church wholeheartedly accepted the ecumenical movement as its own. The restoration of unity among all Christians
became and remains one of the chief concerns of the church. In
fact, as the fathers of the council reflected on the work they had
theretofore accomplished in the council, they could state with
complete justification that "the restoration of unity among all
Christians is one of [its] principal concerns" (1). Pope Paul VI,
in his papal brief declaring the council completed, noted that the
council was the "most opportune" event of the church "because
. . . it has made great effort to reach not only Christians still
separated from communion with the Holy See, but also the
whole human family."

Before speaking directly to this twenty-fifth anniversary
of the Decree on Ecumenism, I wish to spend a few moments
reflecting on the narration about Zaccheus in Luke's Gospel.
"Hurry down," the Lord called out to Zaccheus, "I mean to stay

at your house this day." Immediately upon hearing this, the people began to murmur, "He goes to the house of a sinner." This crowd was no doubt hoping to change Jesus' behavior. Instead, paradoxically, it was Zaccheus who underwent conversion. He stood his ground and promised to the Lord, "I give to the poor and if I defraud anyone in the least I repay him fourfold."

In truth, it is not the crowd which caused Zaccheus to change his heart. It was rather Jesus himself. Jesus revealed to Zaccheus the meaning of the truth of his person: "I mean to stay at your house this day." Zaccheus heard the words of Jesus, recognized what Jesus was saying, and underwent a dramatic conversion of heart.

The house of Zaccheus can be understood to represent the church of Christ. To the church Jesus reveals the true nature of his person: "I mean to stay at this house this day." The conversion of Zaccheus is the conversion of each of us when we understand the meaning of Jesus' revelation: a change of heart that expresses itself not just as a reconciliation with Christ but a renewed unity with others, a renewed conversion of solidarity.

In the Decree on Ecumenism, the council teaches, "There can be no ecumenism worthy of the name without interior conversion" (7). This change of heart, the council continues, "[along with] holiness of life [and] public and private prayer for the unity of Christians, should be regarded as the soul of the whole ecumenical movement, and merits the name, 'spiritual ecumenism'" (8).

What is this spiritual ecumenism? Is it to be understood as distinct from a so-called "material ecumenism"? Does the council intend to set up a dualism between two different types of so-called ecumenism? No. Indeed, to the contrary, the council teaches that there is one ecumenical movement, for there is one Lord, one baptism, one home with Christ, the cornerstone.

Therefore, ecumenism must be rooted in and have as its source the conversion of heart to the one Lord, holiness of life, and prayer for unity. These are to ecumenism what the soul is to the body. They are the locus, the essential place of grace, the *sine qua non* within which the Holy Spirit accomplishes his gift of unity among the churches. It is for this reason that the council teaches that spiritual ecumenism is the soul of the ecumenical movement. It is within the realm of spiritual ecumenism that the Holy Spirit first addresses individuals and churches, calling forth in them an attitude of ecumenism and, once having called it forth, sustaining this attitude within them and among them. It is the Spirit who enables all to be one and the unity to be a multitude.

The council's Dogmatic Constitution on the Church speaks of the church as the people of God. "By giving the Church this conception of itself," our present Holy Father wrote, "the Council at the same time imparts to it an ecumenical attitude in the broadest sense." The Decree on Ecumenism then gives this "ecumenical attitude" a more specific understanding. First, it urges us to maintain an attitude that recognizes our common human identity and solidarity. This identity and solidarity above all have a profound religious sense; that is, they are rooted in faith in the fatherhood of one God embracing one universe and in the universal redemption by Christ, who wills that all come to the knowledge of his truth and of his salvation that he offers to all without exception.

At the same time, this ecumenical attitude must be expressed in a profound love for all, that is, in willing the ultimate good for another, and a respect for one another's inner liberty. Each is endowed with this true inner liberty, calling the other to a responsibility toward the truth revealed in the incarnation of Christ and in the church. In fact, love is authentic only to the degree that it respects the responsible liberty of others, above all in the religious sphere. Thus the church does not seek a forced unity or one that is not authentic in its source and in its sustenance. Rather, the church seeks a unity that is at its deepest level free and faithful. For "the Lord is the Spirit," as St. Paul teaches, "and where the Spirit of the Lord is, there is freedom" (2 Cor. 3:17). As Mohler puts it, each disciple lives out this ecclesial communion "as thinking and desiring in the Spirit and heart of all."

This ecumenical attitude, rooted in faith in the fatherhood of God and in the universal salvation of Christ, sustained by him in the love of the Holy Spirit, furthermore must be lived daily by all Christians and by all churches and ecclesial communities. Accordingly, Christians must seek always for unity in their day-to-day activities—unity with God through prayer and conversion, unity between spouses and among children through mutual reconciliation, unity with friends and neighbors, in workplaces, and in all human associations through faithful response to the prevenient grace of the Holy Spirit.

Having reaffirmed spiritual ecumenism as the "soul" of the ecumenical movement, I now return to the image of Queen Mary I and Queen Elizabeth I waiting in the hope of the resurrection in their tomb in Westminster Abbey. May I first call your attention to the tombs of two other English persons in the Church of St. Gregory the Great on the Coelian Hill in Rome. We recognize this church chiefly as the place from which St. Augustine took his last farewell of Pope St. Gregory the Great for the evangelization of England in the late sixth century. One grave is that of Sir Edward Carne, the ambassador to the Holy See of both King Henry VIII and Queen Mary I. The other is the tomb of Robert Pecham, servant of King Philip and Queen Mary of England and Spain; the inscription on his tomb describes him as unable to look upon his English homeland "without sorrow" (*sine dolore*). Both became exiles for the Catholic faith, unable to return to their English homeland after the Protestant Reformation, and both died in Rome.

In reflecting on these two English Catholic expatriates of the sixteenth century, we come to the realization that one of the special challenges for ecumenists is to summon all Christians to a healing of memories. The metaphor of the two queens, one Catholic and the other Protestant, waiting in the hope of the resurrection can become meaningful only through a mutual reconciliation over the horrific and bloody events of the centuries of division. There must first be a painful remembering and forgiveness and healing. The integrity of the eventual restoration of unity among divided Christians requires it.

Second, continuing differences between Protestant and Catholics over the nature of the eucharist, despite significant convergences in various bilateral dialogues, cannot be dismissed as mere misunderstandings to be resolved with the appropriate hermeneutical tools. The Catholic belief in the eucharist as a propitiatory sacrifice (Council of Trent) or the sacrifice of redemption (Vatican Council II) is not shared by some Protestant Christians. Yet such was the belief of the undivided church of the first millennium. Much of today's dispute in the West over the priest as minister of the eucharistic sacrifice, and the sacramental nature of Holy Orders, can be traced to this largely unacknowledged difference. Consequently, further study on the nature of the eucharist should be high on any Protestant-Catholic bilateral agenda.

Third, the link between the sacred Scriptures and the church needs to be sustained or, where necessary, reinstated in our continuing discovery of the "other," the partner in our ecumenical journey. There is only one unique mystery in Scripture, "the mystery of Christ, prefigured or made present by the event, interiorized in the soul of the individual consummated in glory" (Henri de Lubac). The literal sense of the sacred Scriptures is insufficient. Place must be given to some form of patristic typology because "the mystical interpretation and Orthodoxy will stand or fall together" (Cardinal Newman). The sense of the text of the sacred Scriptures is not found behind the text, that is, in its historical origins, but rather in front of it, that is, in the world it opens up to the believer.

Finally, one of the most intractable problems facing Christians, especially in the West, is what Fr. Yves Congar described as "the great development of ecclesiology . . . in the eleventh century. It is essentially related to Gregory VII." It was the subtle but substantive change in the understanding and exercise of pastoral authority that arose from the crisis facing the church in its struggle with the imperial state. As a result of this conflict, pastoral authority came gradually to be somewhat separated from the preaching of the faith and the celebration of the liturgy. It was an unwitting but serious deformation of pastoral authority unknown in the first millennium. Christians in the West became preoccupied with canonical authority as *dominium* or *potestas,* that is, an authority that dominated or even possessed its subjects, rather than with authority as *ministerium,* the service of Christ in our sisters and brothers. The consequences continue to entangle the churches in all areas and affect all bilateral discussions on papal primacy and infallibility. The exercise of ecclesial authority frequently is filtered through the prism of secular power.

The primary ecumenical agenda facing the churches is the conversion of mind and heart. What we remember on this anniversary is that during our journey with Jesus to Jerusalem through Jericho, he addresses these words to us: "I mean to stay at your house tonight." We recall our response to Christ upon hearing these words, a response involving a fundamental conversion to unity, accomplished by the Holy Spirit not by using pressure or by imposing a uniform pattern on the whole of the church's life, but by the more delicate way of communion. We remember the words of the council, "This Council declares that it realizes that this holy objective—the reconciliation of all Christians in the unity of the one and only Church of Christ— transcends human powers and gifts. It therefore places its hope entirely in the prayer of Christ for the Church, in the love of the Father for us, and in the power of the Holy Spirit" (24). And finally we remember the prayer of Jesus. "Father, that they may be one, even as we are one . . . so that the world may believe" (John 17:11, 21). In remembering, we wait in hope of the restoration of that full unity "through the Holy Spirit which has been given to us" (Rom. 5:5).

The Veneration of Saints as Ecumenical Question

George Tavard, A.A.

The ecumenical importance of the question of the veneration of saints is growing in the USA, especially with the influx of Latin Americans in some parts of the country. It is more than a cultural issue, because Catholics and Protestants have generally been divided on the veneration of saints and its compatibility with faith in "one mediator between God and men, the man Christ Jesus" (1 Tim. 2:5). The division may be looked at historically: what were the opposite doctrines in the sixteenth century? What were their remote or recent antecedents? What were their implications for the central doctrines of Christology and soteriology?

The division was first explicit when Melanchthon included Article XXI among the doctrinal articles of the Augsburg Con-

---

The Reverend George Tavard, A.A., is the author of more than thirty books who, though officially retired from academic teaching, continues to do theological research and continues, as he has for almost twenty-five years, to serve on various interchurch dialogues. Presently he is a member of the Episcopal Church-Roman Catholic Dialogue (ARC-USA). Father Tavard resides at Assumption Center in Brighton, Massachusetts.

fession. The confession was presented to the emperor and the diet on June 26, 1530. A team of some twenty theologians, led by Johannes Eck, assembled toward the end of the month to formulate a conservative response. In the meantime, Zwingli's more radical *Ratio fidei* was presented on July 8, along with the Tetrapolitan Confession on July 11. The *Responsio catholica* was presented to the Catholic estates on July 15 and to the whole diet, in a revised and final form usually called the *Confutatio pontificia*, on August 3. Melanchthon answered in turn with his *Apology for the Confession of Augsburg* (1531), in which Article XXI is longer and more systematic than in either the confession or the *Confutation*. These discussions in fact filled a vacuum, for there had been little theological reflection on the cult of saints between the *Caroline Books* of Emperor Charlemagne (794) and the Reformation.

The question may also be studied in the present context. In the aftermath of Vatican Council II, Pope Paul VI decided to favor the seasonal (Advent, Christmas, Lent, Easter, Pentecost) over the sanctoral (saints' days) cycle in the liturgy. He eliminated a certain number of feasts of saints from the calendar. Yet, with his beatifications of 38 persons and his canonizations of 83, he set a trend that has been followed and amplified by John Paul II. In his first ten years in office the present pope beatified 299 persons and canonized 254. This is the exact number of saints who were canonized by all his predecessors since Benedict XIV (1746)! Early in 1989, Cardinal Joseph Ratzinger, in answer to a question after a lecture given at Seregno, near Milan, wondered if "too rapid a succession of canonizations was judicious," and suggested that priority be given to those potential saints who have a universal message. Given the present return of the saints in force through these innumerable canonizations, one may well ask: What is the present status of the invocation of saints in the Catholic Church? What is the contemporary meaning of canonization? What, if anything, did Vatican Council II say or imply about the cult of saints?

The two points of view, historical and contemporary, are

inextricably linked and share the quality of having evolved without careful theological reflection. The development of an elaborate process for the canonization of saints, the codification of which is essentially the work of Pope Benedict XIV (1740-1758), who, as Cardinal Lambertini, wrote a *De servorum Dei beatificatione et beatorum canonizatione* (1734-1738), was more a reaction against Protestantism than it was the harmonious development of accepted theological principles. The procedure for beatification and canonization was simplified by John Paul II (in the apostolic constitution *Divinus perfectionis magister,* January 25, 1983). Yet over the centuries the church has proffered few magisterial documents about the cult of the saints as such, with the major exception of the *Theotokos* (the teaching of the Council of Ephesus [431] on Mary as the bearer of God).

In this essay, I will focus only on the veneration of saints in general. I will begin with some remarks on the origin of the cult of saints in Christianity. Second, I will examine the problem as it was posed and discussed in the sixteenth century in relation to Article XXI of the Augsburg Confession and the *Confutation*. Third, I will look at the related question of popular religion and devotions. Finally, I will make a proposal toward an eventual ecumenical consensus.

Origin of the Cult of Saints

The historical origin of the cult of saints is well attested. It does not derive from anything specific in the Old or the New Testament. The "witnesses" who form a "great cloud" in Heb. 12:1 are examples of faith, not objects of a cult. The cult is attested at first in relation to the Christian martyrs; their annual commemoration is the occasion for their invocation. Perpetua and Felicitas in Carthage, like Blandina in Lyon, are asked to intercede during their imprisonment for others, with the implication that their intercessions will continue after their martyrdom. Perpetua's intercession is effective even for her little brother who has been dead for a number of years. People and churches are proud to have the tombs of martyrs in their cemeteries. Among the martyrs are the apostles Peter and Paul, and numerous graffiti at St. Peter's and at St. Sebastian's show that their invocation was commonplace for pilgrims in the third and fourth centuries. The standard form of invocation was simply, "Pray for us." One can safely make the hypothesis that the pagan cult of mythological or historical heroes, itself the basis for the cult of the divinized emperor, was instrumental in spreading a certain cult of the martyrs, who were seen by Christians as heroes of their faith. A model for the further growth of this cult was undoubtedly the cult of angels, a belief parallel to the pagan cult of demigods. The growth of angelology and of the veneration of angels is well attested in the Gnostic writings (for example, in the Pseudo-Clementine literature), in which intermediate entities are multiplied. Eventually some of the church fathers (such as St. John Chrysostom) invite the faithful not to pray to angels, while others (such as St. Ambrose) approve their invocation as a private devotion.

There is reason to think that the cult of the Theotokos, after the Council of Ephesus, was promoted in part in order to counteract a spreading cult of angels. At any rate, the struggle against Origenism in the East and Priscillianism in the West includes condemnation of some ideas in angelology. The council of Rome of 745 forbids the invocation of angels on the use of other names (borrowed from the *Book of Enoch*) for angels or archangels than the three scriptural names, Michael, Gabriel, and Raphael. The dedication of church buildings to angels is also declared unlawful. Yet medieval piety encouraged familiarity both with the angels and with the saints in heaven, along with pilgrimages to the tombs of the saints, the cult of relics, and the representation of angels and saints in Christian art.

The Sixteenth Century

That the medieval cult of saints should have been criticized by the Reformers is not surprising, since nearly all existing doctrines and practices of piety were held up for scrutiny in the sixteenth century. But that the division between Protestants and Catholics on the proper place of the saints in piety should have lasted so long is nonetheless astonishing in view of the mildness of Melanchthon's original critique.

Article XXI of the Augsburg Confession teaches that saints should be "kept in remembrance so that our faith may be strengthened." Their "good works" should be an example for the faithful. Yet that saints should be invoked, Melanchthon correctly maintained, cannot be established from Scripture. For Christ is "the one mediator," our "advocate with the Father" (1 John 2:1), and the biblical promise is that he will "hear our prayers," not that the saints will hear them. There is nothing in this article with which Roman Catholics cannot wholeheartedly agree, even if they may wish to add that the invocation of saints can be understood and practiced as not contradicting the one mediation of Christ and that it is, in relation to Scripture, an *adiaphoron*, neither commanded nor forbidden.

The *Confutatio*

In their reaction to the Augsburg Confession, the confutators go much further than this. The heart of their argumentation is their lengthy demonstration from Scripture of a point that is in any case not in question: the believers on earth pray for one another. There is ample scriptural witness for this. But the confutators go on to extrapolate from this to the intercession of the saints in heaven for the faithful on earth: if living saints do pray for the church and its members, so do deceased saints. Moreover, that angels in heaven pray for us is scriptural. And surely, what is true of angels must be true of the saints. This is in fact the extent of the *Confutatio*'s demonstration.

Yet this demonstration is supported by three unproven assumptions. First, the confutators assume that it is proper for the faithful on earth to *ask* the saints to do what the saints do. The invocation of saints as such is not discussed or demonstrated. Once the intercession of saints has been established, the confutators take their invocation for granted. But a much stricter argument would have been needed, for the propriety of invocation was precisely the point at issue: Melanchthon refused to pass from veneration and intercession to invocation. Second, in order to avoid the accusation of undermining the unique mediatorship of Christ, the confutators introduce an untraditional distinction: Christ is the only "mediator of redemption," but the Virgin Mary and the saints are "mediators of intercession." Third, the confutators make an unproven assumption about eschatology: since the saints in heaven are "members of Christ," they must share in what Christ does: "Who can doubt that the saints do the very thing which they see Christ doing? And Christ certainly prays and intercedes in heaven for the Church and the faithful on earth."

In spite of the title under which it was presented in Augsburg, *Confutatio nontificia,* the *Confutatio* has never been an official document of the Catholic Church (it was presented to the diet on the Emperor's authority) and it has never been endorsed by the Roman magisterium. In fact, the notion of "many mediators of intercession" never found its way into the common theology. In standard theology and liturgy, the intercession of saints is not a mediation.

Melanchthon's Reply to the *Confutatio*

In the *Apology for the Confession of Augsburg,* Melanchthon endorses the veneration of saints as "thanksgiving for their gifts and as an occasion to strengthen our faith and to imitate their faith and virtues. He acknowledges that angels and saints intercede for us, but he does not see this as a sufficient reason to invoke them. For even though they pray for the church and its members, there is no scriptural promise that they are aware of the prayers addressed to them, or that their prayers effectively mediate between God and the faithful. Invocation of saints is therefore not justified by the gospel, and cannot be required of the faithful.

Melanchthon, however, goes on to attack the confutators on points that their defense of the cult of saints had not claimed. The transfer of merit from one person to another, he affirms, is a hazardous proposition that finds no support in Scripture. Yet this was no more than hinted, in a quotation from Augustine that provided the confutators' conclusion and was not used as an argument. Melanchthon, however, polemically assumes that the confutators agree with a quotation of Gabriel Biel, the nominalist theologian of the late fifteenth century, which clearly asserts the transfer of merits. He also finds this notion in the formula for sacramental absolution.

Likewise, the confutators had not said that the saints *must* be invoked, but only that they *may* lawfully be invoked: this again was taken from the quote from Biel. In keeping with this polemical line, Melanchthon accuses the confutators of making the saints in heaven not only *deprecatores (Fürbitter)* but also *propitiatores (Mittler und Versöhner)*. Propitiation, as he explains, presupposes a promise from God and a transfer of the mediator's merit. The position of Melanchthon is thus solidly based on soteriology: as there is only one redeemer there is only one mediator (as in Article IV of the Augsburg Confession).

With a good deal of common sense, Melanchthon attributes the origin of the invocation of saints to the secular practice of court life, and he adds that it has been the source of many abuses. Thus there is the peculiar notion, undoubtedly present in some forms of popular piety then and today, that some saints specialize in answering certain types of prayer (St. Anne can obtain money for her clients, St. Sebastian heals the plague, St. George protects horsemen). The slippery slope of abuses is described: "At the beginning one finds the commemoration of the saints. . . . Then their invocation follows. . . .

From their invocation one comes to their images, and these are worshipped and credited with a certain inner power. . . . And the fantastic stories about saints are still worse." Hagiographers invent myths and false miracles. Yet the confutators conceal all these abuses, which had been frequently denounced since long before Luther.

Lex orandi lex credendi

Even with his careful refutation of the *Confutatio*, however, Melanchthon does not identify what I take to be the underlying implicit principle of the confutators' central argument. This is no other than the axiom *lex orandi lex credendi*, or, in the original formulation of the anti-Pelagian *Indiculus de gratia Dei* (c. 431), *"ut legem credendi lex statuat supplicandi."* If a devotional invocation of saints is practiced and accepted in the church, then it must have doctrinal authority. For, as Pope Pius XII argued in the bull *Munificentissimus Deus* (Nov. 1, 1950), by which he defined the assumption of the Virgin Mary, doctrine is not based on devotion or liturgy, but liturgical or devotional practice is authoritative in that it derives from "a doctrine which all the Christian world already knew and accepted." Thus "the *lex orandi* is child, not parent, to the *lex credendi;* liturgy is only the fruit on the tree." In other words, the confutators' position was based on their ecclesiology, an ecclesiology that had no clear criterion to discriminate between the development of practices of piety in the people of God and the actual guidance of the church by the Holy Spirit.

The Council of Trent

The present official position of the Roman Catholic Church on the cult of saints is still that of the Council of Trent. At the end of its twenty-fifth and final session, in December 1563, the council endorsed a decree on the invocation of saints. This was actually done in a great hurry. The last session brought the council to its end by treating questions that had been omitted, or at least had not been resolved, in the former sessions: three doctrinal decrees (on purgatory, the invocation of saints, and indulgences) and seven disciplinary decrees. The haste was due to the general desire to end the council, to the wish of the French bishops to go home on account of religious troubles in France, and to the news that the pope, Pius IV (1559-1565), was seriously ill and could die any day. The decree was composed between November 28 and December 3, 1563, largely under the guidance of Cardinal Charles de Lorraine (1525-1574), archbishop of Reims, who used an earlier document that had been prepared in France for the colloquy of St Germain, in 1562, between Catholics and Calvinists. The decree was discussed at the general congregation of December 2. It was unanimously approved on December 3 by the 217 bishops present.

Even though it dealt with doctrine, the decree was practical rather than dogmatic. The text defended the legitimacy of traditional practices (invocation of saints, veneration of their relics, use of their holy images), but reduced the theological explanation and argumentation to a minimum. It affirmed that the invocation of saints is "good and useful": "We humbly invoke them, and, in view of the benefits one should ask of God through his Son Jesus Christ, our Lord, who alone is our Redeemer and Savior, we take refuge in their prayers, their help and their assistance. It is therefore impious to say that their invocation is against the word of God or is a stupidity." This is not much more than a statement of fact.

A more elaborate explanation was provided for the veneration of holy pictures, Trent endorsing the teaching of the Second Council of Nicaea of 787 on the meaning and use of icons, rather than the restrictive position of the council of Frankfurt (794) and of the *Caroline Books*. Careful attention was paid to the need for proper education and to the repression of abuses. Yet the invocation of saints itself was not seen as an abuse. The adage applied: *Abusus non tollit usum*.

Regarding both the Council of Trent and its contemporary interpretation, one may wonder about the weight we should assign the expression *sanctos . . . invocandos esse* ("Saints are to be invoked"). The Latin form of the verb would generally denote obligation, but it may be taken in the milder sense of legitimate possibility. I take it that the commemoration of saints that is part of liturgical services is, by the very nature of liturgy as the common worship of the people of God, normative. But the invocation of saints by the individual faithful remains, at the council of Trent, optional.

Vatican Council II

In the light of Vatican Council II, however, something else needs to be added today. Neither Philip Melanchthon on the one hand nor the confutators and the Tridentine Fathers on the other approached the question of the invocation of saints from the point of view of the "communion of saints." They did not see *cultus sanctorum* as an aspect of *communio sanctorum*. Yet this is the approach adopted by Vatican II in the constitution on the church, *Lumen gentium*. Chapter 7 ("The Pilgrim Church") speaks of the relations of the church on earth with the church in heaven. In the "communion of this whole Mystical Body of Jesus Christ" (LG, 50), we are told, there have been from the beginning a commemoration of the dead and the offering of prayers for them. There have also been veneration of the apostles and martyrs, along with the Virgin Mary and the holy angels, and prayer "for the assistance of their intercession." To them other holy persons were later assimilated as "saints," and recommended to "the pious devotion of the faithful." Remembrance of these saints inspires imitation of their examples. And there takes place an exchange of "fraternal charity" with them: "Our community (*consortium*) with the saints joins us to Christ,

from whom as from its fountain and head issues all grace and
the life of the People of God itself." The saints are our friends
and benefactors. We give thanks to God for them, and "we
invoke them." At this point, Vatican II repeats the formula of
Trent that I quoted above. It further explains: "Every authentic
witness of love, indeed, offered by us to those in heaven tends
to and terminates in Christ, 'the crown of all the saints,' and
through him in God, who is wonderful in his saints and is
glorified in them."

Luther and Melanchthon were indeed right in insisting
that veneration of the saints must be compatible with the basic
principles of soteriology. But, as the confutators rightly perceived, ecclesiology is the proper context for consideration of
the saints. It is only within the *communio sanctorum* (as both
communion in holy things, *sancta,* and communion of holy
people, *sancti/sanctae*) that devotion to the saints in heaven can
do justice to the authentic doctrine of redemption, salvation,
and justification. For in the *communio sanctorum* all is shared by
all. As Luther tersely affirmed in his *Commentary on Galatians* of
1519 (ch. 3, v. 28): "In Christ all is common to all, all is one, and
one is all."

The Cult of Saints and Popular Religion

Both in its origin and in its development, the cult of saints was
a product of popular piety before it was justified theologically
and approved by the magisterium of the bishops. Furthermore,
it has been influenced at various times by nontheological no-
tions deriving from paganism, from superstition, or simply
from secular ideas and practices. The Christians of the first
centuries adopted and adapted the Greco-Roman practice of
honoring heroes and demigods. This was a phenomenon of
inculturation, of the passage from the original semitic culture
of the gospel to the cultures of the gentility that was being
converted. In this inculturation the Christians borrowed the

belief that the tombs of the saints radiate with the saints' spiritual presence and influence. From the late Roman Empire they inherited the belief that pictures of the saints also mediate their presence (on the model of the pictures of the emperor in official ceremonies). As in popular Roman religion they held commemorative meals in honor of the dead. From the multitude of aeons in Gnosticism there remained a tendency, even among the orthodox, to look for intermediaries between God and creation. In popular Christian piety, angels and departed saints became such intermediaries, especially when miracles could be attributed to their intervention and when they were believed to have appeared in vision to various seers.

But there is an inherent ambiguity in the process of the inculturation of the faith. The development of popular religion has always contained a threat to the heart of the Christian faith, namely to the belief that salvation is only through Jesus Christ, the Word of God made flesh, and that sinners are justified by grace alone through faith alone. For this reason bishops and councils have from time to time, and chiefly in the transition at the end of the patristic period when a further inculturation into the world of the Germanic tribes was in process, warned against excesses. The danger of excesses is to substitute false saviors and pseudo-gospels for the only savior and the only gospel.

Yet there are pastoral opportunities in popular piety, of which devotion to the saints is a major ingredient. Such a piety enabled medieval preachers, both the largely uneducated diocesan lower clergy and the preaching friars, to bring consolation and hope to the poor in terms that used the senses of sight and hearing to reach the mind and heart. It freed the imagination of the simple folk in relation to the divine. It opened up possibilities of visual and oral theologies for those who are not scholars or clerics and even for the illiterate and the uneducated. It bore remarkable fruits in the visionary theologies of medieval women, such as Hildegard of Bingen (1109-1179), Elizabeth of Schönau (1129-1164), and Julian of Norwich (d. after 1416), and in the visual and aurial spirituality of Jeanne d'Arc (d. 1431).

Focusing as they did on the abuses, the Reformers did away with the more problematic aspects of the veneration of saints, notably with their invocation. By and large, however, the Catholic Church, in the past as also today, has not experienced the dangers as outweighing the pastoral advantages. It has opted for the magisterial control of popular religion in general and of the devotion to the saints in particular rather than for their abolition. Whether the control has always been watchful enough is of course a matter for debate. This is not surprising if we also note that until recent decades at least, Catholic missionary projects have generally been more open than the efforts of Protestant missionary organizations to the necessity of inculturation and adaptation.

The contemporary magisterium of the Catholic Church is well aware of this twofold dimension of the question. In February 1974, the bishops of Campania, Italy, wrote a remarkable letter on popular religion with special reference to the cult of the saints. They duly noted the sociological and folk dimensions of this cult. They pointed out a number of patent abuses in their part of the world ("The saints are the object of an all but pagan cult") along with the necessity of a proper renovation of these devotions. And they gave careful instructions on the meaning of "religious feasts, processions, pilgrimages, and shrines."

This was also a topic of reflection in Pope Paul VI's apostolic exhortation *Evangelii nuntiandi* (Dec. 8, 1975):

> One finds among the people particular expressions of the quest for God and of faith. . . . Popular religiosity, one may say, certainly has its limits. It is frequently open to many a deformation of religion, even to superstitions. . . . Yet if it is correctly oriented, chiefly through a pedagogy of evangelization, it contains a wealth of values. . . . It implies an acute sense of some profound attributes of God: fatherhood, providence, loving and perduring presence. It entails inner attitudes that are seldom seen elsewhere to the same degree: patience, the sense of the cross in daily life, detachment, openness to others, devotion.

Accordingly, in July 1977, Cardinal Jean Villot, Secretary of

State of Pope Paul VI, wrote to the Liturgical Commissions of Latin America as they were meeting in Caracas:

> One of the characteristics of the Latin American people is the so-called "popular" religion. This can be the expression of an incompletely informed faith, showing itself in forms that remain marginal to the liturgy, or that reflect cultural and religious traditions from the past. In spite of its imperfections, such manifestations of the faith, taken globally, constitute an authentic value, and it would be a mistake to want to rub them out of the life of the people, especially of the most simple people, without putting anything in its stead.

Given the coming of age of "younger churches" and the birth of autochthonous theologies in Africa, Asia, and Latin America, the inculturation of faith in many cultures confronts traditional Christianity, both Protestant and Catholic, with a major issue. This is a new form of the problem of the sixteenth century: how can the new wine of the Christian faith be preserved in the old skins of many and diverse popular cultures? Should we follow the severe cautions of the Reformers, or share the more humane concerns of their adversaries? The budding dialogue between Christianity and the great world religions raises similar questions: can the Christian faith be in some way grafted onto the religious cultures of India or China?

In contrast with the situation in the sixteenth century, the division today, as we confront the problem of inculturation, would not be between churches. It would be between trends and parties in all the churches. This is apparent in the reactions that have been expressed to the liberation theologies of Latin America. But there is a lesson to be learned from the past: we should not let divisions grow into separations. Some will always be anxious for the purity of the gospel and others for its inculturation. The two sides should not be satisfied with giving different answers to the question, but they should talk and work together for the promotion of the authentic gospel in diverse cultural clothings.

Proposal for an Ecumenical Agreement

In the light of the historic confrontation of 1530, of the summary of the question at the council of Trent, and of the orientation of Vatican II toward a *communio*-ecclesiology, it seems to me that an agreement between Catholics and other Western Christians, especially Lutherans, concerning the veneration of saints is now possible. Such an agreement could include the following points:

1. The soteriological question of holiness ought to come first. There is no substantial difference here. All holiness is God's gift through Christ. Given sacramentally at baptism, the basic Christian holiness is known only by faith, in the Holy Spirit, as one is justified in God's eyes by God's proclamation. It is confirmed in the preaching of the word and the reception of the sacraments. It is not the fruit of works or the reward of individual merit, but it is entirely God's gift. All the faithful on earth are saints in the biblical sense of the term. All those who die in Christ are saints in heaven.

2. The traditional notion of sainthood, however, includes something else besides holiness, namely the assumption that God has chosen some among the faithful for a particular mission that may be called, analogically, prophetic. This mission lies in that their life, as it is known and remembered, should illustrate some aspect of the fullness of God's gift of holiness. Many whose prophetic life is particularly remembered have been proclaimed "saints" in a special way.

3. The proclamation of these saints presupposes that means are available to assess the prophetic dimension of Christian lives, and to protect the faithful from mistaken attributions of prophetic tasks, and from excessive or misoriented enthusiasm for specific saints. In earlier times, public knowledge and spontaneous veneration were operative. More recently, the process of canonization that has been institutionalized in the Catholic Church relies chiefly on the evidence of heroic virtue and on the recognition of miracles attributed to a saint's prayer. Whether such signs of holiness are sufficient or convincing

remains a matter for debate. The opinion that canonizations by the bishop of Rome are infallible proclamations of "dogmatic facts" is untenable, as it does not fit the requirements of Vatican Council I for the exercise of papal infallibility.

4. It is certain that all the saints in heaven, the mass of the holy people as well as the canonized saints, pray for the church on earth.

5. Because the saints of the church triumphant pray for the church militant, the veneration of saints has inspired the simple prayer to them, "Pray for us," which expresses remembrance, trust, love, and solidarity, in keeping with the nature of *communio sanctorum* as the communion of the whole people of God.

6. Apart from joining in this prayer when it occurs liturgically, the Christian faithful have no obligation to pray to specific saints, although in practice many do so, in keeping with their personal devotion. There is no reason to believe that specific saints ought to be invoked for specific purposes (as in the case of the Fourteen Auxiliary Saints of late medieval piety).

7. One of the tasks of the ministry is to protect and promote the purity of the gospel in the forms of popular piety that result from the inculturation of the Christian faith in the many cultures and civilizations of the world. Fidelity to the Scriptures implies respect for the normative role of the semitic culture that is embedded in them and for the exemplary experience of hellenistic inculturation in the early church. And the success of the missionary proclamation of the gospel requires sensitivity to the hidden action of the Holy Spirit in all cultures and religions and careful study of the providential potential of all cultures.

Be Transformed and
Become a New Creation

Thomas Hoyt, Jr.

We remember the unity that we have in Jesus Christ and we pray for the unity that we seek with each other as we mark a giant milestone for the Christian churches, one reached twenty-five years ago when the Second Vatican Council issued the Decree on Ecumenism. Fr. Thomas Stransky, C.S.P., one of the original staff (1960) of the now Pontifical Council for Promoting Christian Unity, has rightly stated that even though the vision of Christian unity is variously addressed today, negatively and positively, its "genie" has been released from the bottle never to be rebottled again. The proof of this is easily seen in the commonplace manner in which ecumenical happenings occur.

Some things become so commonplace that we take them for granted. But this place where we gather—Howard University School of Religion—the composition of this audience—Protestants, Catholics, and Orthodox Christians—and our

Thomas Hoyt, Jr., is Professor of Scripture at The Hartford Seminary, Hartford, Conn., Vice-Chair of the Faith and Order Commission of the National Council of Churches, and a member of the Faith and Order Commission of the World Council of Churches.

celebrating a happening by Roman Catholics is providential and miraculous and should not be taken for granted.

It is fitting that we celebrate the Decree on Ecumenism because the church unity movement has come a long way from what it once was. Symptomatic of the weather during the birth of the Decree on Ecumenism was the climate of the world during the sixties. Let me illustrate from my own life. Born in the 1940s in Alabama, to parents in the Christian Methodist Episcopal Church; living and worshipping in black churches from my youth up; eating in cars when we took trips because we couldn't sit at a restaurant or check into a hotel when we got tired—these are but signs of a divided and segregated America. It wasn't until the 1950s when I attended a meeting in Columbus, Ohio, of the Student Christian Movement that I began to see blacks and whites working, studying, and worshipping together. It was in the 1960s that I saw blacks and whites, Protestants, Catholics, Orthodox, and Jews marching together, singing together, going to jail together, eating together. I saw ecumenism at its best in the streets of America in the sixties. In a sense our gathering of blacks and whites, Protestants and Catholics, to mark the twenty-fifth anniversary of the Decree on Ecumenism is a mini-repeat of those events.

What people were doing in the streets—getting together —was facilitated by laws in America against segregation and discrimination. Action in the streets brought awareness and transformed America. Appropriately enough, on November 21, 1964, the Decree on Ecumenism facilitated a dialogue intended to provide impetus for relationships and communion with other confessions or fellow Christians not a part of the Roman Catholic Church.

Transformation in society and transformation in church go hand in hand. The committee who planned this observance displayed insight when they chose the Scriptures and the subject for our reflection:

> I appeal to you, therefore, brothers and sister, by the mercies of God, to present your bodies as a living sacrifice, holy and

acceptable to God, which is your spiritual worship. Do not be conformed to this world but be transformed by the renewal of your mind, that you may prove what is the will of God, what is good and acceptable and perfect. (Romans 12:1-2)

And now I am no more in the world, but they are in the world, and I am coming to thee. Holy Father, keep them in thy name, which thou hast given me, that they may be one, even as we are one. (John 17:11)

I do not pray for these only, but also for those who believe in me through their word, that they may all be one; even as thou, Father, art in me, and I in thee, that they also may be in us, so that the world may believe that thou hast sent me. (John 17:20-21)

Now there are varieties of gifts, but the same Spirit; and there are varieties of service, but the same Lord; and there are varieties of working, but it is the same God who inspires them all in every one. To each is given the manifestation of the Spirit for the common good. (1 Cor. 12:4-7)

In John's Gospel, Jesus offers a high priestly prayer for his immediate disciples and those who would believe as a result of their words: that they may be one even as he and the Father are one so that the world may believe. In Romans, Paul stresses transformation and reconstruction through renewal of the mind so that one might be able to place one's body on the line in the service of God and others. In 1 Corinthians 12:4-7, Paul perceives that the body of Christ functions best when it is free enough in the Spirit to allow all to use their gifts for the good of the whole body. These three passages together simply say that we must begin to present our bodies and gifts for the service of transformation into a unified, reconciled community, a new creation. The Decree on Ecumenism recognized that there is no true unity without transformation of mind and giving one's all to the service of God and others.

The aims and successes—and failures—of the Decree on Ecumenism, rather than dampen the quest for unity, have heightened the pressure from the ecumenical movement, which more and more compels Christians to dialogue, common prayer, practical collaboration, and common witness.

The prayer of Jesus in John recognizes that there can be no proper dialogue, common prayer, practical collaboration, or common witness unless one is properly situated in communion with God. The prayer of Jesus simply says that the church that would be one must know its identity, and to whom it belongs. The church belongs to God, not to the values of the world. In praying for the disciples, Jesus prayed (vv. 13-16):

> But now I am coming to thee; and these things I speak in the world, that they may have my joy fulfilled in themselves. I have given them thy word; only the world has hated them because they are not of the world, even as I am not of the world. I do not pray that thou shouldst take them out of the world, but that thou shouldst keep them from the evil one. They are not of the world, even as I am not of the world.

It is significant that a fundamental characteristic of the disciples' existence in the world is joy. However, that joy does not include the assurance of peace, security, and worldly pleasure, for the disciples will experience tension and hostility at the hands of the world (v. 14). Far from being comfortably at home in the world, they are not of it. So their peace and joy is of another order. Their joy and peace is the quality of their life in fellowship with God through Christ. In the black community the song we sing is true to John's gospel: "This joy I have, the world didn't give it to me. The world didn't give it and the world can't take it away."

To say that the church does not belong to the world does not mean that the church is not to be for the world. Despite their alienation from the world (vv. 14 and 16), Jesus does not ask that his disciples be taken out of this world. "World" here is the world that people create by their alienation from God. Therefore rejection of this world is not the rejection of the created order or of things material. Moreover, God loves the world, even in its alienation from him.

Jesus does not pray for the world directly, since "world"

in John means the unbelieving humanity, and to pray for the world would be to pray for the hardening of the world in its unbelief, to pray for the world to be "world," to be more entrenched in its worldliness. But since the church, as we hear in verses 21 and 23, exists precisely in order to bring the world to faith, this prayer for the church is indirectly, by detour, also a prayer for the world, "which God so loved"—in fact, the only appropriate kind of prayer for the world that there can be: that the world may cease to be "world" in the Johannine sense that it may cease to be in unbelief and come to faith. A church in prayer for another value system than one sees in this world is the essence of the prayer of Jesus.

Because of Jesus' praying for the unity of the disciples and the church that comes after them, we may ask, "In what does this unity consist?" It is grounded upon the unity of Jesus Christ and his Abba. It is an incorporation of the believers into that unity ("that they may be in us"). The unity of the church is therefore no purely social or organizational phenomenon. Neither is it solely a matter of agreement on doctrinal or other matters. Unity involves a union of the many beings in the one being. John must be interpreted very carefully on this point. He does not speak of the absorption of souls into the one soul or the wiping out of individuals. Individual personal identity is maintained within this union. In this union the Christian attains a new status, if not a new being.

How is one to carry out the requirements of this prayer of Jesus that we become one? Paul suggests that we need a reconstructed, transformed mind and the utilization of gifts of the Spirit. First, let's say something about sacrificed bodies and transformed minds. Paul said, "I appeal to you, therefore, brothers and sisters, by the mercies of God, to present your bodies as a living sacrifice, holy and acceptable to God, which is your spiritual worship. Do not be conformed to this world, but be transformed by the renewal of your mind, that you may prove what is the will of God, what is good and acceptable and perfect." "Present your bodies as a living sacrifice," exhorts St. Paul, echoing the most profound and simple truth spoken by his crucified and risen Lord: "They who seek to find their lives shall lose them, and they who lose their lives for my sake shall find them." We present our bodies as living sacrifices, we serve as ministers: prophets, teachers, workers of miracles, healers, helpers, administrators, ecumenists. We do so withholding nothing of ourselves and for ourselves because Christ lived, because Christ withheld not Christ's self. To the ultimate degree not required of us, Christ presented Christ's body as a living sacrifice for us all. As we follow Christ, miracles do happen and have happened in the ecumenical world. Sometimes our bodies are literally sacrificed by drafting documents in the ecumenical movement on behalf of the ecumenical world. Miracles of understanding and ecumenical relationships only happen when we do not become like the chicken and the hog who, after having discussed what each of them could give for breakfast, saw the hog balk at the chicken's suggestion that if the hog would give some ham, she would give some eggs. The hog replied: "No way can I give ham! For you to give eggs is a sacrifice but for me to give ham demands total commitment." As an ecumenist, one must be willing to be a different kind of hog, giving total commitment—giving one's whole self.

A transformed mind is required in order to be fully committed to unity of the church for the life of the world. It was the genius of the Decree on Ecumenism that recognized the value of transformation. First, if one wanted a transformed mind, one had to transform one's vocabulary. The decree sought to eliminate negative and unfair words, judgments, and actions toward others. The writers knew that words affected behavior. This desire for change has been partially fulfilled in Roman Catholic catechisms and textbooks as well as in homiletic and liturgical language.

Second, the decree sought to facilitate transformation through dialogue between competent representatives of various churches. If one would relate to any structure other than one's own, one needed to know what the other was thinking. One need only recount the many international, national, and local dialogues between and among churches to show the relative success of this intention of the decree. In the various dialogues every major doctrinal subject has been touched upon, but moral ones have barely been approached in joint discussion. Issues that divide, such as abortion, homosexuality, divorce and remarriage, are hardly mentioned in joint communiques. Why? Partly because the various dialogue partners are not nearly ready to deal with these matters with their own family members. When alliances on these issues occur they are usually between Protestant fundamentalists and conservative Catholics on such issues as school prayer and abortion.

Third, the decree wished to foster transformation of mind and society through cooperation in public activities for the sake of the common good. The 1960s coalition of persons for justice organized across religious and denominational lines. But since then, the struggle for justice has usually been carried out by Catholics and Protestants doing their separate thing, whether through pastoral letters or denominational statements on nuclear warfare or on the economy. In spite of the lack of initiative to foster cooperative work in the justice arena, the drafters of the Decree on Ecumenism were wise in recognizing that real unity is impossible without real transformation in the public arena.

Lastly, the decree aimed for transformation through common prayer. This aspect of the church's life has not been fulfilled. It can still be said that Sunday mornings are the most segregated hours in American churches, socially and religiously speaking. Archbishop Stafford called our attention to another issue on which almost no progress has been made: intercommunion, especially eucharistic fellowship. Since these matters are taken up elsewhere in this work we do not need to dwell on our lack of a mutual recognition of each other's ministry, which is largely owing today to the issues of ordination and the role of women in the church.

The Apostle Paul, in addition to calling for commitment of one's whole being as a transformed person for the life of the world, calls also for using the gifts given by the Spirit in the service of transformation and a new creation. The gifts of God are for the people of God.

God gave us all a gift in Pope John XXIII. That gift has continually been nurtured by the Vatican's Pontifical Council for Promoting Christian Unity. Pope John Paul II personally has nurtured the quest for Christian unity because he sees it as a pastoral concern.

It is through Protestant, Orthodox, and Roman Catholics meeting and giving their bodies as "living sacrifices" that we see today a change of mind and an exchange of gifts that we cherish. We should be committed to a continual sharing of those gifts that have been developed by those who have presented their bodies as living sacrifices in the service of transformation and a new creation.

We must continue to recognize the truth of the witness of the Word of God which tells us that unity is a gift rather than mere human effort. The unity of the church, because it is a mystery and an act of God, will not result from the plans of men and women, even though we must plan. Unity will come in moments of surprise, in unexpected places and ways. We plan for unity, knowing that the results are ultimately in the hands of God.

Deep commitments in ecumenical contexts call for the gift of sharing pain. In the most ordinary circumstances it takes summering and wintering to trust each other with our stories of pain. But in bilaterals and multilaterals, in global and ecumenical contexts, trust emerges slowly out of a movement away from parochialism to ecumenism. In sharing painful stories of disunity our vocation is to listen, touch, respond, and care.

Attending a meeting of the World Council of Churches, I was pained, along with others, when a member of a sister church announced to us that it would be impossible for them to give us communion—although if we thought them wrong, they invited us to pray for them. They then proceeded to give communion to each other. After the real thing was over, the rest of us were offered bread that had been blessed and would be shared as a sign of brokenness and as a sign of hope. The gift of sharing pain is a gift that will be all too common in the days ahead. But we must struggle on in hope.

Continual commitment to the ecumenical task calls for the gift of sharing in creative encounters with worship. Worship that is built from the traditions, the liturgies, the music, and the languages of many faith communities has about it a whole earth quality, one that transcends the one-note parochialisms of our life. We must learn anew what the Decree on Ecumenism affirms, namely that spirituality is at the heart of the ecumenical movement. For example, "spirituals" of the black tradition and gospel songs are understood and appreciated in various cultures. Even at the Faith and Order meeting of the World Council of Churches in Stavanger, Norway, one was keenly aware that music transcended cultural lines. White youth in that setting knew and could sing the gospel music of André Crouch better than I myself.

A particularly cherished gift in ecumenical settings is listening and responding to multiple voices, reflecting the accents of different thought forms, doctrinal histories, cultural experiences, and languages. This means that authentic ecumenical communities are always in the tension of potential creativity or loss of creativity. It is demanding, fatiguing, and essential work in the pluralized human community generally and to the church of Jesus Christ in particular.

Yet, this gift of listening to the many voices in one's midst is necessary if we are to bring into being the new community that the Book of Revelation proclaims has already come because of the work of the Lamb. Revelation envisions a multiethnic, multilinguistic, multinational, multiracial lamb whose blood has been shed in order that people from every tongue, tribe, and nation of the earth might be ransomed. Black Catholics in their church talk about a rainbow coalition, much as Jesse Jackson talks about it. Yet, the rainbow coalition that belongs to Jesus Christ, the Lamb of God, far surpasses that of any human institution.

Every branch of the human family—women, blacks, hispanics, persons with disabilities, those of the world community—are making their unique contributions to an understanding of the diversity of the people of God. We are slowly coming to recognize that the family of God includes all nations and cuts across divisions of race, class, sex, and creed.

The real question facing the church in its quest for unity, mission, and liberation is: Can human beings find a unity in the gospel that preserves their gifts of diversity and their distinctive qualities, but that overcomes their idolatries? That question awaits an answer.

Lastly, commitment to the ecumenical movement brings with it the gift of friendship. This follows the pattern of Jesus, who told his disciples, "No longer do I call you servants, for the servant does not know what the master is doing; but I have called you friends, for all that I have heard from my Father I have made known to you" (John 15:15). The call is to recognize the value and rewards of friendship, with love being the overriding concern. Friendships take time—walking time, time at the table, idle time, time to savour common experiences, along with worship time. As we live with ecumenical friends, experiences of "my house" and "your house" move toward "our home." Orthodox, Protestants, and Roman Catholics have had mind-changing experiences because of friendships shared in dialogue. Through these commitments we will be transformed and become a new creation sharing our gifts of the Spirit for the life of the world.

Allow me to close this message with a dream.

I dream of a church that will not become one with the world because of its power, but that has a strong influence in it because of its integrity—a church that can command the respect of the powerful and give them a new vision of a world of peace and justice.

I have a dream of a church that will be in truth a community where God is known, where faith is not just an intellectual exercise but the fruit of the experience of grace.

I have a dream of a church where the ecumenical fellowship of scholarship will continue to provide the basis for documents like BEM and faith statements and actions that make for unity and transformation of individuals and society.

I have a dream of a church that will be truly inclusive,

where the faithfulness of ministry is shared by women and men, rich and poor, liberal and conservative, educated and unlettered, black and white, handicapped and those who do not consider themselves so to be. I dream of all of us being one in Christ Jesus.

I lastly have a dream of not only an inclusive community but also a caring one, working to meet human needs, where living the gospel will be the highest priority.

Jesus prayed for his disciples who were arguing and debating about seats and conflicting understandings of messiahship and kingdom. He wanted them to keep their vision straight. The envisioned church, the transformed church, the new creation, should not allow human jealousies and personal agendas to disrupt the mission of the kingdom. Let's accept each other with all our weaknesses and failings, and encouraged by God's grace, move forward together in the service of Christ.

Walk together, children, don't you get weary. There's a great camp meeting in the bond of unity, justice, and peace. Amen.

Afterword: The Path We Followed and the Horizons We Face

David Trickett

A bittersweet experience connected with the Washington symposium at which the first six papers in this book were presented was a deep sense of loss brought on by Albert Outler's death. He had eagerly accepted an invitation to speak at the event and had been working for some time to craft an address that was intended not merely to provide historically acute commentary or even check the pulse of current relations between Roman Catholics and Protestants a quarter-century after Vatican II's Decree on Ecumenism. Outler wanted also to give some creative nudges to a process of mutual edification and self-discovery that he believed warranted renewed vigor. Would that he had lived to be with us; his passing shortly before his scheduled participation in the symposium deprived all the conversation partners of a much-needed contribution to their continuing discussion. Even as we mourned his death at the gathering, however, we

David Trickett, Executive Director of the Washington Theological Consortium and the Washington Institute of Ecumenics, is an educator and administrator from the United Methodist tradition.

were able as Roman Catholic and Protestant siblings in faith to celebrate together Outler's life and witness to Christian unity. Albert Outler has been one of those brave and genuinely wise souls who has helped to guide the ecumenical journey in a way as to make events such as this Washington symposium continue to be possible—and, we pray, to bear fruit.

Upon the conclusion of our symposium, Thaddeus Horgan and I began to work on the task of making our findings available to a larger audience than we could accommodate in Washington. We wanted to supplement the major addresses and responses with other pertinent contributions that could enhance our invitation to Protestant and Roman Catholic Christians to see that all of us have a shared call to "walk together." I was among the great number of persons shocked and saddened by Thaddeus's sudden death. I lost a friend and colleague who was not only a leader within his own religious community and the larger ecumenical arena but also an eager and active member of my theological organization's board. It is appropriate that the hope-filled glimmer in the eyes of Outler and Horgan—two tireless advocates of the search for unity who have been snatched from our midst—ought to be remembered explicitly in the context of their last public task and the nexus of issues that led to the Washington symposium.

We stand at the threshold of a distinctively new period in ecumenical life and thought. The principle organizations traditionally looked to for ecumenical leadership have been beset by difficulties that have begun to undercut the potency of their collective witness. Albert Outler called attention to this phenomenon several years ago in a vivid reference to the ecumenical "vessel" (the image of a simple boat has been a popular ecumenical symbol for some time): it is still in the water, but it certainly isn't moving as it once did. What was generally overlooked in press coverage of Outler's remark was his firm conviction that ecumenical fervor is certainly as strong as it has been in recent decades—indeed, it may have become stronger—but that its locus has shifted. Whereas many of us have come of age in a day when ecumenism shone at international and national levels, the profound energy and hope of people at a local (and to some extent regional) level is where a powerful vision for the future may now lie. As a member of the community that has long provided a stimulus for the annual "Week of Prayer for Christian Unity" celebrations in this and other lands, Thaddeus Horgan resonated well with Outler's discerning view.

When Thaddeus Horgan and I found ourselves working in the same metropolitan area we both sensed that our shared commitment to community-formation and our awareness of the changing dynamic of ecumenism called for some public outlet. The opportunity that seemed particularly promising was provided by the Roman Catholic hierarchy's celebration of its bicentennial in the United States—which coincided nearly exactly with the quarter-century anniversary of Vatican II's Decree on Ecumenism. Calling attention to the two celebrations and to the ways in which one might fruitfully inform the other has begun new rounds of conversation that may yet prove significant.

Beyond the shift of ecumenical focus that is presently underway, we wanted also to address the withdrawal of increasing numbers of men, women, and youth from confessional religious participation in Protestantism and Roman Catholicism alike. We view this reality as a crucial element on the horizon that ecumenical thought and work simply cannot afford to underestimate. A growing number of people find religion in general—not only theology—no longer engaging. Explicitly confessional traditions do not provide this diverse group of people with a sense of worthwhile participation in something significantly greater than themselves. Some of us suspect that theological education itself may be partly responsible for this dis-engagement process. By emphasizing the nature and shape of clergy leadership at the expense of identifying the ministries of the laity, some very important links fail to be formed. Connections between the worship life of a community and the everyday lives of faithful people need significant attention, and quickly. We need also to broaden the base of participants who help foster a fresh confessional and ecumenical ecclesial identity within and among our respective traditions. Thaddeus and I saw an extraordinary possibility: in the region of the nation's capital, the community of ten theological schools and their constituencies that formed the Washington Theological Consortium could begin wrestling afresh with the challenge to strengthen a Christian understanding of the public significance of ecumenically sensitive theology and lived community witness. The Washington symposium checked to see where Roman Catholics and Protestants had once been over against one another and noted how far we have come together since 1964. The event prepared us to look ahead.

Seeing that we do indeed share some horizons is itself a step forward. Where might we now move? I suggest that we ought not only to continue to affirm the importance of the highly specialized ecumenical discussions that have brought us to the brink of a new millenium but also to embrace the new face of ecumenism—local communities of conviction whose clergy and laity engage one another with renewed respect and trust. Let us not flinch from the further realization, to which both Albert Outler and Thaddeus Horgan pointed us, that once we start to address the real daily concerns of our people we will find ourselves in a whole network of relationships and conversations that even a few years ago may have seemed either impossible or inappropriate. Such alliances can help us deal with issues such as the use of information systems as means of community empowerment and participatory citizenship; human responsibility for environmental integrity; the urgent need to identify and train new generations of leaders in the corporate, public, and philanthropic sectors of society; and the promise and perplexity of scientific and technological advance in fields such as genetics. The horizons before us are vast; the major life-engaging issues now requiring the marshalling of Protestant and Roman Catholic theological vision and ethical principles are transconfessional. We have been led to a place where we pause to celebrate the distance we have already come together. Let the voices of Outler and Horgan continue to guide us, to embolden us, as we look ahead to the next stage of our journey together.